DRAMATISTS
OF TO-DAY

EDMOND ROSTAND

In his uniform as an officer of the Academy.

DRAMATISTS
OF TO-DAY

ROSTAND, HAUPTMANN, SUDERMANN,
PINERO, SHAW, PHILLIPS,
MAETERLINCK

*Being an Informal Discussion of their
Significant Work*

BY

EDWARD EVERETT HALE, JR.

SIXTH EDITION, REVISED AND ENLARGED

WITH PORTRAITS

Essay Index Reprint Series

BOOKS FOR LIBRARIES PRESS
FREEPORT, NEW YORK

First Published 1911
Reprinted 1969

STANDARD BOOK NUMBER:
8369-1261-6

LIBRARY OF CONGRESS CATALOG CARD NUMBER:
79-90639

PRINTED IN THE UNITED STATES OF AMERICA

PREFATORY NOTE TO SIXTH EDITION

THE present edition of this book is an attempt to keep it as near its title as may be. There was immense temptation to make over the whole book. In our own language alone there are several new and interesting phases of the drama that one should say something about, if he is to be in touch with his time. But, on the other hand, the older men are still alive: even the last theatrical season in our country with " Chantecler," " The Blue Bird," " The Thunderbolt " reminds us that they are still leaders. So I have not tried to make a new book, nor even to revise the ideas, opinions, estimates of the old book. I have tried to bring the book up to date by adding such comment and fact as seemed necessary after the passage of five years.

Three or four passages in the following pages appeared originally in *The Dial*, which used to give me opportunities to write on these matters, for which I have always been grateful. I have not thought it necessary to break the continuity by quotation marks or acknowledgment. Ultimately it is due to the indulgent kindness of the

iii

editor of *The Dial* that these papers came into
being at all, and where there is so much general
obligation, it is not important to note a few particular paragraphs.

E. E. H., Jr.

CONTENTS

A NOTE ON STANDARDS OF CRITICISM

OF old a " Critick " studied the masters in any given form of art and thus learned the rules of that art. He might then consider whatever came to his notice and pronounce it good or bad. We commonly do much the same sort of thing now, when we read merely for fun. We have, every one of us, got together, consciously or unconsciously, some ideas on what's what as to novels or short stories or plays or pictures, and when we read or hear or see anything, we instinctively form some judgment of it according to whatever those ideas may be. The process we perhaps express by saying, " I don't pretend to know anything about criticism, but I know what I like." Whether we acknowledge it or not, we commonly form our opinion about current books and plays on some such basis.

This mode of judgment, still popular with the general reader, was abandoned by many brilliant critics some time ago. It seemed foolish to compare indifferently artists of all countries and ages, to call Shakespeare a barbarian because he was not Sophocles, or Sophocles an old grandmother because he was not Shakespeare. And with the growing idea of natural development in every line of human interest came that form of criticism which seeks to explain every work of art by the circumstances, which views it, not in and by itself, but in its coming to be. The idea has taken all forms: Herder in Germany, Mme. de Staël, Chateaubriand, Sainte-Beuve, Taine in France developed the idea, not only as applied to the character of any individual artist, but as the expression of the spirit of national life. Morelli immensely influenced the modern criticism of painting by bringing the matter down to the psychic and physical habits and powers of any given artist, and there have been many minor efforts to do the same thing in literature. The main idea is in all cases the same: the work of art —picture, poem, play—is the result of certain forces; if you would rightly understand the art, first get at the forces. This view may seem to be historical or scientific rather than critical; if everything is just what it had to be in the due course of nature, can we call one thing better than another? Taine was extremely ingenious in offering an answer to this question.

The world was getting rather accustomed to this idea when it was called upon to accept another. Ruskin proclaimed that art was a teacher, and drew away after him a third part of the art-lovers of the world into a place whence it has been hard to escape. In time it appeared, however, that it was not especially necessary that art should be a teacher: the significance of the earlier criticism of Walter Pater lies in the fact that he saw .that art was an active factor in human life. This is so obviously the case—indeed Hazlitt had assumed it a century ago—that it was natural that the idea should be carried to its logical conclusion by somebody. Anatole France presumably came upon it himself, for it is the most natural accompaniment of his delightful effort to reduce everything to $0 = 0$. And others have developed the idea with great effect, notably Mr. Berenson, who, having found out to the uttermost jot and tittle how Italian art came into existence, now goes on and tells us what it was and has been to the world, and what it may be to us.

The drama is more a personal than a theoretical matter. Every one goes to see plays; every one is in some way or other affected by them. In most cases the effect will be no more than comes from a period of rest to a spirit wearied by the rest-

less work or play or ennui of life from day to day.
A relaxation, a recess, a recreation; such is the
theatre to most. But even as such it must be
something more. If this man always does one
thing and that man does something else, they will
certainly differ in time. If one man commonly
goes for an evening's amusement to so-called
vaudeville, and another for an evening's amusement commonly goes to see Shakespeare (supposing he has the chance), there will surely be some
difference finally, other things being equal, between the two. The theatre is too powerful a stimulus for any spirit at all sensitive to escape it
wholly. Let us look at its possible effects.

This, at least, is what I commonly find myself
doing. No one will entirely avoid being dogmatic
or descriptive; no one will avoid some thought of
environment or influence or development. But the
main thing is the effect upon the spirit. I shall
not of course emulate the example of Ruskin, with
his notion that art is didactic and that one must
become as a little child at the feet of prophets,
who at the present day are as apt to resemble
Hosea as Isaiah. Nor shall I follow the steps of
the charming arch-sceptic of our time, which lead
to that void of absolute zero in which his spirit
bathes with such obvious refreshment. I remain
on an isthmus of a middle state. Somewhere about

halfway between the holy mountain and the abyss do I mount beside the puppet booth and give, as though a barker, some comment on the dramatists of our day.

From such a standpoint no one will expect broad and comprehensive surveys; the real pleasure and stimulus in a mountain view, say, or indeed any other view, does not consist in a mastery of all the details; it is something very different. A delightful landscape charms one at the moment and makes itself thenceforward an influence in the mind, so that one is happier at one or another moment for the thinking of it. So it is with other things in life, and especially with art; one is immensely struck by a picture, it may be, and it remains in one's thoughts a long, long time, having part in all sorts of unknown psychoses; one hears music, and a melody or a phrase stays by one, often running in the head in very trivial fashion, but often serving finer ends. To discern and analyse these things is something that criticism has hardly tried to accomplish, but it is certainly a thing to be done. The purists always think they can tell you what correct pronunciation ought to be, but it is really necessary, first, to know what everyday pronunciation is. Before one can lay down the law as to how one ought to feel about a drama, it is but reasonable to try to find out how one really does feel.

And this is somehow not a very easy matter: it would seem as though people after a play preferred to think rather than feel. It is not very difficult to think about a play that one has seen or read, and that may be the reason that most people do so. But note theatrical criticism and see how little consists of impression, save in the most general terms, and how much of knowledge, opinion, gossip. It is true that one must have a good deal in the way of facts and recollections; the impressions made by a play upon a mind like Locke's white paper will not be of much interest in a complex civilisation. One must do a good deal in the way of description and analysis of character, construction, situation, for that is often the only way that one can present one's impressions, and those things are immensely interesting and valuable for themselves or in relation to other criticism. Still, they are not the main thing here: if they were, I should have to apologise for many omissions and, I suppose, not a few commissions. No one, I hope, will carp at my neglecting academic system and completeness. I have so much lecturing on literature from day to day, so much of the academic way of looking at things, that it is really a means to mental health to do

something else. There are many other dramatists
of our day who ought to have their part in any
real treatise on the current drama. From the
ferocious Strindberg on the north to the equally
ferocious d'Annunzio on the south, from the symbolic Mr. Yeats on the other side of the water
to the late Mr. Clyde Fitch, whose cymbals tinkle
rather differently, there are several dramatists as
interesting as some of whom I speak. And then
there is Ibsen; no one can neglect him, nor, indeed, have I done so; for although Ibsen is not
precisely a dramatist of our day, he is a remarkable influence on the drama of our day. To us in
America Ibsen belongs to the past or to the future,
surely not to the present. And since there are many
books and essays on Ibsen, I have thought it as well
not to attempt any new estimate of his work. In
fact these papers make no attempt at a complete
and systematic view. In trying to form such a
view of the work of our time, much of the freshness
and spontaneity would be lost, and even then the
game would not be worth the candle, for in a few
years something would turn up that would make
what had been systematic seem very desultory.
Current criticism should, I suppose, result from
something pretty definite in the way of ideas, but
I doubt if it need result in anything definite in the
way of system.

A play presents its material to us in a concentrated form attained by certain devices which, though literary in character, are usually developed from the necessities of the stage of the period. When the play is actually presented on the stage, its effect is heightened by many devices which are not literary in character, as acting, stage-setting, and so forth. It is interesting to note these devices, these ways in which the impression is made upon us, to point them out, to talk of them. There is an immense amount of very interesting stuff here; indeed, it makes the greater part of technical dramatic criticism. But it is all only means to an end; the real end is that we ourselves shall be affected somehow or other by the play. If we are nowise affected, or affected in a way we dislike, we might as well stay at home; or if we are at home reading the play, we might as well read something else or nothing at all. Our interest in these contemporary dramatists is that we get something from them.

This something, in the case of a play of any value, always lasts for a while, perhaps a day or two only, perhaps merely during supper after the theatre, but generally longer. To state precisely the general nature of this effect in simple language is not at all easy; I do not know that it has ever been very systematically analysed. Neglect-

ing, however, such accidents as a sweet smile, a
phrase of music or of words, a beautiful dress, we
may say that we shall usually have in mind a bit
of human experience. This experience may be, in
its general circumstance, familiar to us, as in
" Candida," or it may be quite unfamiliar or even
impossible, as in " Die versunkene Glocke," but
human experience it is, or it does not remain long
with us.

Just what we do with this new possession will
differ according as we differ, but the main things
that we do will be one or another of these following. We may deal with it as we should with any
piece of real life, laugh or cry over it at the time,
think about it and talk about it afterwards as
though it were real. How was it with Mrs. Tanqueray? Was it right or wrong that the world
should have used her as it did? Our views on
these matters may very probably be influenced by
the dramatist, but we commonly neglect that consideration and think and talk as we should of real
people. Or next, we may be pleased with something in the play because, though not real life, it
is such an absolute resemblance of it. Miss
Prossy, for instance, and " Prossy's complaint "
will give a thrill of pleasure because they so perfectly resemble something that may not in itself
be so very interesting to us. It is very fine, we

say, because it is so true. Thirdly, this human
experience may concentrate itself, as it were, in a
figure or situation that will appear to us to imply
or signify something of importance, which figure
or situation will recur to the mind at one time or
another with a good deal of the original feeling
with which we first experienced it. This is one
reason why Mme. Bernhardt is such a powerful
ally to any dramatist: she readily makes herself a
dramatic figure.

This last process, I rather think, is the most
specifically connected with the drama. The first
is a little naïve; it reminds one of the many stories
about inexperienced persons in the eighteenth century or in frontier towns or early in life, who
thought that the play actually was real life. It
is something which has no especial connection with
the drama; it may occur well enough with any
form of representative art just as it may with life
itself. The second is a great pleasure undoubtedly; it has been noted by many an analyst before and after Pope; still it gets from the drama
only what one may get from all literature and all
graphic art as well. The last seems to me the
pleasure particularly dramatic, for just this
result the drama is particularly fitted to give by
all its especial powers and devices, and to quite
the same degree no one of the other arts can give

it.   Something of the kind we have from painting
and from fiction and poetry, but the drama combines the powers of the two.   It gives us figures
for the eye and for the imagination at the same
time.   To have such impressions is in itself an
æsthetic pleasure of the purest kind.   What results from it is another matter.

ROSTAND

When M. Edmond Rostand became a member
of the French Academy, he was accepted as a man
of letters of the first rank by a body which has
made mistakes, but still holds the respect of the
world. His reception was therefore an event. I
read that even from the outside of the Palais de
l'Institut one could " measure all the importance
of that ceremony." To perform that feat, my
authority continues, it was enough, at least for
an observer well up in his " Tout Paris," to see
the people going in and coming out; the different
persons of importance in " les mondes littéraire,
artistique, scientifique, aristocratique, diploma-
tique," who formed groups " d'un charactère sug-
gestif et d'un interêt documentaire." Not being
very strong myself in " Tout Paris," I must confess that the only one of these groups presented by
l'Illustration that was of real interest to me was
that consisting of M. Rostand himself in a cocked
hat and a cloak, with a sword sticking from under
it, preceded by an usher. And from a consideration of the other groups, I incline to think that the

importance of the occasion may be measured, perhaps, but not fully estimated, by a consideration
of the persons who were present at it, although it
is of interest to be told that there were more guests
than there have been at any such occasion in the
last half-century.

In fact various writers have estimated the significance of the event in a totally different manner.
They have considered it as bringing forward the
question of M. Rostand's position from the standpoint of literature.

From the standpoint of literature it will be ob-
served, rather than from the standpoint of the
theatre. For it seems obvious that a man need
not have any position in literature by virtue of
theatrical masterpieces alone. Other positions he
will have thereby, but not a position in literature;
for that one must produce books that people will
read. Literature is a matter of letters rather
than of sounds, one may say. A man may be a
great talker, but only rarely does one gain a place
in literature by conversation alone; Boswells are
too rare. One may be a great orator, but even
so, one is known in literature by the printed form,
as when Macaulay wrote out his speeches, ten and
twenty years after he made them, not in the precise words he had used, which were irrevocably lost.
but in words which he might have used. So with

the dramatist. If his work have anything of literature in it, it will be something that will stand the test of type.

The theatre, undoubtedly, produces often matters that are most delightful when put in book form, but the theatre, as such, is not concerned in that fact. Of the innumerable forms of the drama, many have little about them that can be called literature,—melodrama and farce, as a rule, the clever extempore drama of Italy and other lands, the pantomime which often has a strikingly dramatic quality without a single word, and, we may add, the now extinct Weber and Fields burlesque, which seems to have been a theatrical genre of great interest to the student of the stage, in its possibilities at least.

This matter is clear enough to the keen-eyed critics of M. Rostand's own country. They looked upon his reception into the Academy with interest, because, as they said, although he had dominated the purely theatrical criticism, he had not, up to that time, wholly won over the critics of literature. " If the people of the theatre can hardly speak of M. Rostand without a sort of amorous emotion in the voice, literary people have been able, on the contrary, to make him the subject of a more unmoved criticism." Such at least was the view of M. Gustave Kahn, who went on to consider " la

valeur littéraire " of the author of " Cyrano "
and " L'Aiglon."

I must leave M. Kahn to his own opinions, for
it is surely none of my business to controvert or
agree with the ideas of a French critic on the
position in French literature of a French dramatist. But the point is noteworthy in this way: M.
Rostand had a great success, out of France at
least, for reasons that were somewhat non-theat-
rical, or that were at least supposed to be. In
Germany the critics, at least, laid stress upon his
ideas and in this country something of the sort was
the case. Not that it was not delightful to see his
plays at the theatre; not that, had he presented
his ideas in other forms, they would have been as
successful as they were; neither of these supposi-
tions is the case. But given the theatrical success
of M. Rostand, a thing that he possessed in common, for instance, with Mr. Clyde Fitch or Mr.
David Belasco, that which was the staying quality,
outside of France at least, was the literature and
not the extreme theatrical skill.

Of course many of those most ready or competent to speak on this subject are of a very different
opinion. But what will you have? A man cannot
be always thinking like other people, he must wan-
der off by himself sometimes. And if, in such wan-
derings, his views are false or foolish, the best

thing to do is to speak them out, for then he will
be corrected by those who are wiser. So I offer
my view of the literary element and quality in the
work of M. Rostand with perfect cheerfulness,
even though it is very different from that of—well,
various people of consideration. And there is certainly pleasure in looking over the work of M. Rostand, as though he were not a successful playwright who may be seen (let us hope, again) at the
theatre, presented by the most charming or the
most dominating of the actresses of the day, but
rather—what shall I say?—rather as though he
were one of the great dramatists of the literature
of the past, whose work is now withdrawn from
the glare of the footlights and enclosed silently
between covers, for the delight, not of the ground-
ling or the man from the street, but of the pale
student under the midnight bulb or the member of
a popular literary club.

In M. Rostand's first work for the stage, " Les
Romanesques," he was surely attractive, but not
very much more. A writer who thinks that in that
charming little play we have M. Rostand " tout
entier, où il est le meilleur, dans la picaresque
et la funambulesque," seems to miss so much
suggested by the later plays that one is tempted
to ask: Is it really there, all this that we think
moves us? or can it be that we are reading into

the work of the poet ideas which were nothing to
him and thereby neglecting the very things that
were in his own mind the real ones? Yet I shall
for the moment believe that it is not so, and go on
to say that " Les Romanesques " is not what might
be expected of the author of " Cyrano de Bergerac." Not because it is slight, nor because it is
little more than attractive, but because it is a delicate satire upon the tribe of romancers in general.
Percinet and Sylvette, two young people who live
on estates separated by a high wall, are full of a
fine desire for colour, and beauty, and charm. They
long for a wonderful life and condemn the commonplace. Their fathers appreciate their disposition, too, and, not unwilling to pose a bit themselves, they affect to be bitter enemies. The lovers
are transported into the seventh heaven and become Romeo and Juliet. How can they be united?
They suggest ridiculously impossible plans, and
then their fathers humour them with a scheme of
their own. It is delightful while they think it
genuine, but when they find out that they have been
tricked they are enraged. Sylvette refuses to be
married and Percinet goes forth to seek for adventure in the world. Of course he returns and the
play ends happily, as the saying is.

M. Rostand's great triumph was in romance.
Is it to be said that to begin with a burlesque on

romance and to succeed with a romantic triumph shows a lack of sincerity?

That is not just the way to put it. Men do not often jest at what they deem great. But they do jest (and often very bitterly, as Rostand does not) at the world's perversions of what they deem great. Rostand believes in romance, let us say, but he has his laugh at the romancers. Did not Sir Walter make fun of Julia Mannering?

These charming lovers are doubtless silly; they think they must have exquisite mystery, recondite sensation, something strange, out-of-the-way, fascinating, anything in short that they have not got. But so it is also with their everyday fathers: they also think they will be satisfied with what they have not, but when they have it, Pasquinot is bored at Bergamin's watering pot, and Bergamin is bored at Pasquinot's always having a button off his waistcoat. Youth is one thing, age is another, but both, in so far as they substitute dreams for reality, are fair food for wit.

But what is reality? And here Percinet speaks possibly for M. Rostand.

" It was real for us who thought it real.

Sylvette. No. My being carried off, like your duel, was all made-up.

Percinet. Your fear was not, madame."

The mind that is sincere makes the reality, but

people are too ready with the conventional commonplace as with the conventional romance. Romance itself may be real enough if it only be real romance and not the conventional, the make-believe, the fashionable. Percinet on the road, Sylvette in the garden, learn that life is not made up of phrases and attitudes.

This was the thing that the Realists and the Naturalists and the rest had always had in mind. They had laughed at the old romance and its costumes and properties, its phrases and attitudes. They themselves presented truth. Now Rostand is by no means a naturalist, still he loves truth, only he would present truth differently: the realists presented truth by its ever-varying myriad circumstance, Rostand would present it by its essence, its idea, its type. Hence " La Princesse Lointaine."

In " La Princesse Lointaine " we have the idealist, the ultra-romantic Rudel, faithful to the very door of death to the Princess whom he has never seen. But we also have the Princess, too, and she is not faithful. She fondles the idea of an absent lover devoted to her image, and when she hears from the redoubtable Bertrand that her lover is at hand sick to death, awaiting her on his mattress laid on deck, she will not go to him. And why? The subtle Sorismonde suggests a reason. " You will not see him who was dear to you in the divine splendour of a dream, because you would not see him in the horrible haggardness of the fact; you would keep the recollection of your love still noble."

"Ah, yes!" says the Princess, "that is the only reason."

But it is not really the contrast of the visionary love and the haggard fact that moves her. It is the contrast between the imaginary love and the actuality of the passion that she feels for the messenger. Sorismonde tells her that she passes from a dream into real life. She says herself that she denies the pale flower of the dream for the flower of love. But when the experiment is made it appears that the flower of love, that the actuality of life, has been bought at too high a price, that there was something even more real in the imagination, in the dream, in the romance. Squarciafico cannot understand such a thing when it occurs in his own humorous accompaniment to the lyric motive. He grasps it no better than the average realist. "But I am opening your eyes!" he says to the sailors. "And suppose we prefer to keep them closed?" they say in their blundering faith, not differing much from many readers of Zola. It is only when she has given up the passion of actuality, and returned to the old ideal that she believed in, that Melissande finds herself on firm

ground.   At the end she knows the one thing
needful.

"La Princesse Lointaine" was not successful
upon the stage, I believe, and it is not wholly convincing here and there when one reads it. That
goes rather without saying. Had it been a first-
rate play, M. Rostand would have been famous before "Cyrano." There is much that is beautiful
in "La Princesse Lointaine." The indomitable
hero, the faithful sailors, the audacious quest, the
intensity of the moment of action, and a very exquisite reconciliation to the tragic end remain in
one's mind and may well outweigh a lightness and
over-refinement of handling. At least one is impressed with the feeling that here is one who can
say his word on the deep things of life and give
his imagining the form of beauty. And here is a
word spoken with no uncertain voice for the power
of romance.

As to "La Samaritaine," that is certainly a
matter rather hard for the average Anglo-Saxon
to handle. It is hard to understand the mental
attitude which conceived the play. It is of course
not the simplicity which presented much the same
thing five centuries before, in the mystery plays.
But then it is hardly the balmy scepticism with
which another Frenchman, some time since, offered
the world a Galilean idyl in exchange for an

inspired Gospel. However we take it, though,
we have a play made from an episode in the career
of the greatest idealist the world has ever seen.
To my ears, however, all that rings true in the
play is that which reminds me of words otherwise
long familiar. The play has lately been given a
few performances in America by Bernhardt.

It was at the very end of the year 1897 that
" Cyrano de Bergerac " was produced and at once
achieved an immense success in Paris, and not very
long after, throughout Europe and America. It
was a great day for Romance, a second " Hernani."

In the history of the literature of the nineteenth
century Cyrano de Bergerac will be a well-remem-
bered figure—would be something much more than
that, except that people do not read plays as much
as they read novels. But even as it is, Cyrano de
Bergerac is, and will remain, one of the great
figures which the French literature of our time
offers the world. As we look back, any one of us,
into the vista of our earlier days, and recognise
the figures that arise from the readings of our
youth, the first to strike us, when we think of our
early acquaintance with French literature, is the
figure of the heroic d'Artagnan. Or is it Consuelo? Never mind—the elder Dumas and George
Sand were the great French writers of our earlier

days, as they were of an earlier part of the century. It must have been later in life that we became acquainted with the Comédie Humaine and Marguerite Gautier, with Madame Bovary and the Rougon-Macquart family. Whether it were so or not in our own individual youth, it was practically so with the youth of our time. To readers nourished on Byron and Scott, France gave the " Three Musketeers " and " Monte Cristo," " Mauprat " and " Consuelo." Then came the turn of the tide, and a generation brought up on Dickens and Thackeray and George Eliot put aside childish things and were thrilled by the tragedies of Balzac, Dumas fils, Flaubert, Zola. Of course there were other realists, too,—realists everywhere,— but these were the men who represented France, and who created the typical characters that seize the imagination and recollection of all.

Then, as the century was coming to an end, France presented another figure,—and that not realistic, but romantic again,—presented it to a world that was ready to enjoy romance once more. Just as a generation fed on Scott welcomed d'Artagnan, so a generation fed on Stevenson welcomed Cyrano de Bergerac. The pendulum had swung back.

When, after the duel in the first act, a brilliant and heroic musketeer strides out of the crowd and shakes the victorious Cyrano by the hand and disappears, the incident is more significant than the audience appreciates. " Who is that gentleman? " says Cyrano to Cuigy. " It is M. d'Artagnan," says he, and Cyrano turns round; but the older hero is gone, and Cyrano holds the attention alone. The two are alike and are different. Both are heroes who fire the old-time savage element of the soul,—Gascons, swordsmen, indomitable, men of the compelling word and the convincing stroke, hot-blooded, honourable, heroic. But there is also a difference: one is striking, brilliant, magnificent, and the other is almost grotesque. He is cruelly grotesque; there is nothing to lighten it; it is nothing one can pity, like a hump or a club-foot; nothing one can delude oneself into thinking fine, like a mountain belly and a rocky face or a Rochester sort of hideousness; nothing that one can fancy is significant, like a birthmark or a distorted mouth. All these things the world would forgive or forget. Here is something ridiculous, something that would make any of us shiver and writhe if we saw it by our fireside. Here is something that touches us cynical, susceptible, bantering people, touches us in a very tender place.

And yet one swallows it, and with it all minor matters. Cyrano might, by an enemy, be called a bully and a braggart, but that possibility is quite lost in our general sympathy. We do not think of that any more than of his nose; we feel only that he is a noble figure. This is rather a curious thing. It is the result of Realism, I take it. In the old, old fairy tale, the beast stopped being a beast when he was loved. The monster became Cupid. But Realism pricked that bubble, and we recognise to-day even in literature, as a rule, that human nature is, and will long continue to remain human. We must accept the strange mixture of the god and the animal. We must recognise that the old-time dreams are dreams— beautiful, encouraging, inspiring, to be remembered and to be thankful for, but not truths that we shall ever know. Realism fixed upon us the pre-eminent thought of our time that the triumph of the spirit is despite the flesh, and the new Romanticism profited by the lesson. Our English romancers—Mr. Stanley Weyman is a good example of a hundred—did not quite dare. They were conscious that their heroes must not be the old-time impossibilities, but they compromised, as a rule, by having their heroes chumps, stupid though well-meaning, and of course successful at the end. They did not dare to go to the impossible extreme which so often makes the type. M. Rostand did dare to do so, and succeeded.

Is it a curious thing this swinging over to Romance? We used to think that romance was something for children. They read about d'Artagnan fighting duels or Ivanhoe in the tournaments, while their elders read (aloud) Anthony Trollope's accounts of everyday life reaching the culmination of excitement in a rattling fox-hunt. And then suddenly we found that the tide had turned. Not suddenly, perhaps, for long ago I remember my inward wonder when a man whose taste I esteemed told me of his joy in "King Solomon's Mines." No, it was not sudden, for no change in taste is sudden, but it was sure nevertheless, so that it is perhaps not the less curious.

Still we may ask, Is the new Romance the same as the old? Is Scott the same as Stevenson? Is "Cyrano" the same as "Hernani"?

Certainly Stevenson is not Scott. He is not so large a man for one thing, but for another he is not of the same kind. So far as real life is concerned there is no comparison, Scott is the only one to think of. But so far as romance is concerned, there is little enough comparison either. Incomplete as Stevenson is, powerless often to express his own convictions, he never tried to present figures as empty of real significance as the Master of Ravenswood and the Disinherited Knight. He sought for the romance of the spirit and not for

the external romance of costume and circumstance
that satisfied Scott. In fact, Realism has had its
effect, for it has made people more serious.

Cyrano is surely a character for the playwright.
" Mais quel geste," he says. It surely was a good
attitude,—just why who can divine?—that throwing the bag of crowns on the stage. Nor was Cyrano ever at a loss for such attitudes. He is quite
without affectation when he sets forth to march
through Old Paris at the head of that strange
procession of musicians and soldiers and actresses, as well as when the Spanish officer asks:
" Who are these so determined on death? " he
replies: " These are the Gascon cadets! " and
charges the crowd of Imperialists with the few
that are left.

Such things are characteristic of him. He must
do them. We cold-blooded creatures do not understand such things. They seem perhaps sense-
less to us and foolhardy, we do not know what
they mean. This melodramatic character thrills
us perhaps, but we cannot sympathise because we
cannot interpret. To us Cyrano is an actor, and
we Anglo-Saxons are not individually apt to act,
nor to respect the actor as such. So we miss one
side of the man, one of his perfectly natural means
of expressing himself.

Only this one side, however, need we miss, if that

to some degree. For this dramatic expression so natural to Cyrano, as I suppose to all French and many more, is but one side of the character. It is a mode of expression for certain things, but not for everything. There are things about Cyrano that do not come to such expression.

We Anglo-Saxons want ideas or we think we do. All else we put aside as being superficial, insincere, and so miss the greater part of the dramatic spirit of the Latin. But Cyrano has his ideas, too, as well as his poses. He is less conscious of them perhaps, but he has them, or rather, as we should say of his poses, he is them.

Cyrano is in fact a type—a type of the largest class of people in the world (for it includes every one), namely those who do not get what they know they deserve, who find no chance to do what they know they could do, who are so much greater to themselves than to the cold world. He is also the type of a much smaller class who do not make a fuss about the matter, but carry it all off so gaily and finely that no one has any consciousness of complaint, murmuring, repining; indeed perhaps there is at bottom hardly a suspicion of anything of the kind. From the girl who is not like other girls, from that strange commercial traveller some years ago who published poems that his friends might know his real self, to the philosopher with his " To be great is to be misunderstood," or to the professor who fretted and fumed and lamented, and tormented himself " because, as he acknowledged to himself, the Thou sweet gentleman was not sufficiently honoured," to the great Queen exclaiming: " If my people only knew me as I am!" we all nurse an ideal in our hearts and most of us know that it will never be realised, even that it cannot be realised. For one reason or another, doubtless,— not always a nose,—perhaps even it is the necessary nature of things, though that is rarely the view that we take of it.

And so Cyrano takes our sympathy. We are even as he. With him it is a nose, with us fortunately a something else, that prevents our standing forth to the world for all we are worth. This, besides many minor matters, good each in its own way, is the thing that unconsciously touches all.

Yet, because M. Rostand is not Shakespeare or some one like him, we do not have everything. Some would say because he is a Frenchman, decadent, pessimist, morbid, he has nothing more to say than just that. Here is a man who was fine, strong, brave, good, and never got his due. What of it? Well, the rest is silence, or nearly so. The last act is pathetic, touching, but not illuminating. Certainly Roxane did not love him, —or suppose she did, what of it? He had no comprehension of it. And suppose he had had, what then? Would that have been what we feel the true, the inevitable end? I fear not.

Still it is a beautiful play. To-night, seven years after I read it first and saw it on the stage, I read it once more, and that with some misgiving. But the beautiful verse has lost none of its beauty; the gaiety and verve and spirit have lost none of their lightness; the situations have lost no thrill; and the play has much the same meaning as that first night when I read it, and it pursued itself through my mind till morning,—as much and more.

When a man does something very fine indeed he may well fear—or at least his friends may fear for him—that he will not be able to do something else worthy of being compared with it. Until we get used to it, genius so often seems accident. There must be some high wave that no other wave will reach. When M. Rostand had surprised the world with "Cyrano de Bergerac," it was not unnatural that the world should suppose that the next play would not sustain the effect.

Such doubts were set at rest on the appearance of "L'Aiglon," when the book was read, and doubly so when the play was seen. Many thought that M. Rostand had bettered his masterpiece.

This tragedy, with its poor, weak little hero, with all its frivolity, all its decadent circumstance, made a stronger effect than its wonderful predecessor—stronger, if less obvious.

As before, we have under very special conditions a figure of general appeal. This young man, yearning after that great inheritance which he hears, which he feels is his, imagining it in all sorts of glittering and deceptive circumstance, treasuring scraps of others' reminiscences, gaining hope from misinterpreted detail, indulging his fancy with aimless triviality, daring in ill-advised effort,—for he hardly knows just what, —failing and surrendering himself to the inevitable currents of life and even death,—he is not for us particularly the young Napoleon, he is merely what he essentially is, a poignant example of the fate that stands ready for all humanity.

"L'Aiglon" was first produced in New York not long after a revival of "Hamlet," so that it was not unnatural to think of the Prince of Denmark in his weeds of customary black while looking on the French prince in his Austrian white. Without comparing M. Rostand with Shakespeare, we may still compare the great figure of English romanticism in its heyday with this later figure of French romance. It is perhaps singular that in an age pre-eminent for exuberant conception and

fulfilled achievement the greatest creation of literature should have been the man who thought
too closely on the event, and kept on living to
say, *This thing's to do,* until circumstances took
the matter out of his hands. Not less singular is
it—if either be singular at all—that at the end
of a century of unrivalled material achievement
should appear this presentation of the prince who
strove to realise his fancies and failed.

So M. Rostand is not merely a Romanticist in
the sense that he gives us rattling sword-and-
mantle plays, in which things happen, according
to the saying of the day. He is that sort of neo-
Romanticist whose figures are types—a romancer,
we may think, of the school of Hawthorne. And
his figures generally typify the same thing.
Rudel is the poet whose love for the ideal leads
him to his own death, happily unknowing of the
reality which is nearest him. Cyrano is the
average man, perhaps, though one of immense
talent, the man who sees what he really is, what he
really might be, perhaps, but reconciles himself
slowly to the impossibility of ever making the
ideal conquer the world. And the Duc de Reichstadt surely is an idealist of the first water. No
confident holder of the faith in the presence of
undeniable fact was more determined than the
Duke as he listens to Metternich and finally breaks

the mirror. He, too, gives way to the fact of the matter, but he is broken and not bent.

What is it that leads M. Rostand to this presentation of invariable failure? Is it because he is morbid, cynical, pessimistic, etc., etc., etc.? Hardly. It is due to something far more general than such possibilities, namely, the tragic quality of great drama—I had almost said of great literature. In spite of all that has been said about the agreement of literature and life, there is this singular and important difference, that literature is in its greatest moments tragic, and that life is not. M. Rostand writes as he does because he is a dramatist, a poet, a man of letters, and not a pastor, a philanthropist, or a philosopher. As such he cannot present the world as being all delightful and right in the end. No great poets while they were great have done so; Job, Helen, Hamlet, Don Quixote, Faust, Colonel Newcome,— these all are tragic figures.

I cannot pretend to explain, from the standpoint of æsthetics, why this should be so. The frivolous (and I am often one of them) will say that every story must have an end, and that death is the only end that will stay ended, among matters of importance. Minor matters certainly come to an end, as clothes, for instance, the best even of dinners, light loves in the portal. But with the really important things it is different. Marriage, of course, often plays the rôle of conclusion, on the stage or in the book, but it is one of the unrealities of comedy that it does so. Look about for an end, and you will find it hard to think of any but death or disappointment, which, if it be really an end, is much the same thing.

Without taking this view too seriously, we shall perhaps admit that it is not for literature to demonstrate that things are going all right. That seems rather the office of philosophy (if it wants to try it) or of religion. Literature is for our emotions. Now happiness is emotionally delightful, but by its very nature it is not permanent. "Even in the very temple of Delight, veiled Melancholy hath her sovran shrine," said Keats, with that direct, far-seeing intensity of his. While man is what he is, mere satisfaction can never be final. And however this may be in art in general, or even in literature or in poetry, it is readily enough seen to be so in the drama. Comedy certainly is delightful, but the great things are tragic. And that is because a great dramatic moment, one that will remain with us, be permanent, must be complete in itself—that is to say, final. Now Romeo and Juliet in the tomb of the Capulets are final figures. So Hamlet as he utters "The rest is silence." So Lear on the

heath, beyond even the power of Nahum Tate.
Comic figures there are also, but one cannot bear
to think of Falstaff always laughing. Romantic
figures there are too, suave and beautiful. Ferdi-
nand and Miranda, as they play at chess, and
certainly we should like to believe them eternal,
but the appeal is very *ad hominem,* and the wise
will take it for no more than it is.

So Cyrano throwing his bag of money on the
stage is a permanent figure. " Quel geste," he
says, feeling the thing to the bottom, but without
troubling to analyse it. So L'Aiglon breaking
the mirror is a permanent figure. So Rudel on
the deck of his galley.

These figures give us dramatic moments. But
they also mean something, and we Anglo-Saxons
are dead set on seeing what they mean. " The
most popular play of the final decade of the century presents no problem whatsoever, and avoids
any criticism of life," says a critic of eminence,
as though it were a fault. Mme. Bernhardt and
M. Coquelin, however, see that these things
have their meaning for those who appreciate them
and never think of explaining. So M. Rostand.
He contents himself with dramatic figures. They
justify themselves. Explanation belongs to the
philosopher.

To reflections such as these, and others of all

sorts and kinds, Rostand left his admirers and
friends for a long, long time. He did not take
any place in the literary world, save as being a
member of the Academy, he did not even remain
at speaking distance. He retired with his family
to a country place in the Pyrenees and there remained in secluded consideration of whatever he
thought worth while. An occasional paragraph
about him appeared in the papers, but nothing
by him. He was, as it were, like Shelley's poet,
" hidden in the light of thought." He was unlike
Shelley's ideal, however, because he did not sing
his hymns unbidden till the world was wrought to
sympathy with hopes and fears it heeded not. He
gave nothing to the world at all, and the world
talked of him now and then, read gossip and criticism about him, looked at pictures of him, bought
his plays by the hundreds of thousands, wondered
what he was writing, but was not wrought to sympathy with him because he remained silent.

It was almost ten years to a day before the
silence was broken by the production of " Chantecler." Had this remarkable work appeared un-
heralded, it is impossible to say what would have
been its reception. As it happened, some knowledge of the play and its subject had long been
abroad, so that the public mind was far too much
absorbed in fancy and conjecture to be able to

form a frank and natural opinion. Not very long
after " L'Aiglon " a subject had occurred to M.
Rostand. The idea of an animal-play was suggested to him by the old French beast fable, the
Roman de Reynard; a conception not of animals
and men, but of animals only, like the fables of
Æsop and much else in the literature of the world,
more especially of La Fontaine, so familiar to the
French from school days up. A farmyard with
its glorious rooster had suggested to him the Gallic
cock as hero, and he had forthwith surrounded
himself not only with all literature that might
inform and stimulate, but with all the essentials
of the barnyard itself. In a year or two the play
was substantially written, but there supervened all
sorts of delays. Illness and consequent doubt had
led him to be doubtful of his work and to turn
to other subjects, of which two characteristic ones
are mentioned, Don Quixote and Punchinello. But
neither of these had held his attention long nor had
illness been able to distract his mind permanently
from his work. In time the play was so far com-
pleted that the actor Coquelin was summoned, for
whom the part of Chantecler had been conceived.
The play was gone over by poet and actor, and
the questions of stage presentation were gradually
discussed and solved. Then occurred a sad disappointment: Coquelin, who had seemed destined by

eternal fitness to take the part of Chantecler, suddenly died. But this obstacle, like all others, was
surmounted, and the play came finally to performance. It had seemed to one at a distance that it
was simply impossible that the poet of " Cyrano "
and " L'Aiglon " could create anything worthy of
mention in the same breath as those masterpieces,
out of the idea of a cock in a barnyard. If anything, it could be nothing but a tremendous *tour-
de-force.* All sorts of ideas were held on the subject
all over the world, for according to modern ideas,
the play was preceded by the most immense amount
of (unsolicited and unpaid) advertisement, so that
everybody had heard about it. The result was
better than might have been imagined. " Chantecler," though taken as a whole it was not so fine
a piece nor so great a success as its two great
predecessors, was certainly a play of very great
beauty. In some respects it was extravagant, and
it was not so readily suited to the stage, but in
other ways it was easily superior. It may be
doubted whether the judgment of time will not
pronounce it Rostand's greatest play.

It would appear at first that no poetry and no
significance could render tolerable a play in which
all the actors strove to give the appearance of birds.
The nose of Cyrano becomes insignificant when we
imagine such incongruities as are necessary. What

possibilities of sympathy, tenderness, love could there be in the relations of a man dressed as a cock and a lady clad as a golden pheasant? Here perhaps the reader of the play might have some advantage over one who should see the extravaganza on the stage. But even on the stage such expectation was disappointed; the effect was beautiful, harmonious, artistic. The absence of man in the dramatis personæ, and the reduction of the size of the actors by the larger size of all the surroundings of barnyard and woodland, put things into a relation which was not only correct enough, so far as the actors were concerned, but which somehow isolated the scene and made the barnyard a world of itself, in which the conceptions of the poet could affect us without the intrusion of ideas extraneous to it.

On the face of it, then, the play was a charming extravaganza concerning a splendid rooster of the barnyard and a golden pheasant of the woods. Their love works itself out in the midst of a great world of animal life far more varied than would have been possible in the more familiar world of men and women. The various hens and chickens, the ducks and turkeys are there, the watchdog, and the cat asleep on the wall, and the bird in the cage. There are also some less usual inhabitants, the peacock, the guinea-hen, and a vast array of

cocks of all races and climes. There, too, are
others, owls and hawks and pigeons and guinea-
pigs. There are beings of the wood—it is need-
less to name all who take part—night-birds, toads,
frogs, rabbits, cicadæ, the woodpecker, the nightingale. All these make a most brilliant spectacle,
and one which might easily have been amusing
enough to have carried a whole play. What sort
of action beyond the simplest would have been
necessary to carry along such brilliant possibilities
in the way of costume and setting?

M. Rostand, however, would hardly have been
likely to present so simple a conception. His cocks
and pheasants, his blackbird and watchdog, his
ducks, bees, frogs, owls, nightingale, are as in
the fable types of humanity and his play presents
forms and phases of human life. And here he has
the fabulist's advantage, namely, that having
merely the typical forms,—the simple-hearted,
beautiful poet, the wild gipsy of the woods,—he
can keep his attention close to the main idea without being diverted to personalities and circumstances. One's attention is not distracted by little
realisms as in the case of plays of men and women.
If he had tried to present really a poet and a
free child of nature, his main idea might easily
have been overgrown by all sorts of little matters
necessary to the presentation of character, and yet

impertinent to the main idea. It had been so, indeed, with both Cyrano and L'Aiglon: each had been a real living man who had by his very reality and vitality obscured the idea which the poet had so strongly felt in his creation. It was not so with " Chantecler ": such little verisimilitudes as we have of the real cock and hen, are of the slightest of humoresques. Chantecler himself is felt first and last to be the poet who rejoices in the influence of his song, the pheasant hen is the eternal feminine who has at this moment acquired the brilliant garb of the male, the blackbird in the cage is the satirical cynical man of the world, the dog is the rough and faithful friend, the guinea-hen is the fussy, empty-headed woman of society, and so on. Each figure bears its part in the general extravagance, but each is also an element in the fable of the Poet and the world.

Here Rostand shows himself to be an interpreter of life as well as a poet. Was it that he felt that no one had heretofore seen that in all his plays before he had been saying his say about life in general? Not only had he been telling stories of Gascons, troubadours, heirs of destiny, but also presenting life as a chance to play the game for all it was worth. Probably he had no such feeling: Rostand appears to be singularly uninfluenced by the criticisms of the world. He expresses himself as he feels is right. It may be that now he felt that what he had really had to say had fallen on the ears of people too desirous of sensation and excitement to listen for the soft, clear note of wisdom. At least he presents a man who believes that the world is called to life by his song. Through all temptations—the attacks of the world, the assaults of love—he remains true to his conviction. Finally tempted out of himself by a beauty beyond what he has himself dreamed, he finds that in his own forgetfulness of his mission the world has gone on its own way without his help. What he thought was Life responding to his song, appears to have been a course of events rising from other, far greater causes. Chantecler believes that it is his clarion note that calls the sun and brings the day. Were it not for him, all would be dark: nature would sink into a perpetual sleep. A golden hen pheasant tempts him to the silence of the wood but cannot win him from his constancy to an all-forgetful passion for herself. But what she cannot do is done by another. Chantecler hears the nightingale: listening in absorbed rapture to her wonderful song, he forgets to sound the note that shall arouse the sun. The sun rises, however, without being aroused, and Chantecler wakes from his dream of beauty to be undeceived as to fact.

It is in this situation that Rostand shows himself somewhat different from the dramatist of " Cyrano " and " L'Aiglon." So far as power and poetry are concerned the three plays are on the same plane. Probably the superiority in beauty and brilliancy will in time, if it be not already, be awarded to " Cyrano de Bergerac." But " Cyrano," as well as " L'Aiglon," suffers, as has already been said, from a sort of inconclusive character. Cyrano in the after years, the Duc de Reichstadt in his sick-room, are neither of them satisfying figures. Chantecler is at the end finer than at the beginning. Like Cyrano he is brought to see that the ideal cannot conquer the world at a stroke, like the Duc de Reichstadt before the mirror he sees that he is not to be the master of the world. But Cyrano passes quickly out of the world of achievement, and the unhappy Duke is broken if not bent. Chantecler is neither. If at first his ideal was overweening, there is still something for him to do. The last we hear of him is a victorious " Cocorico," as he goes back from the seclusion of the forest to the realisms of his little world.

HAUPTMANN

TEN years ago, say, the name of Gerhardt Hauptmann was a magic name; it was almost a charm in itself to cause the most glorious æsthetic thrills. It represented the finest things in literature. It is now rarely heard. " So sinks the daystar in the ocean bed, and yet anon flames in the forehead of the morning sky." There is fortunately time, though not so much as once.

Hauptmann, however, never achieved such immediate, such inordinate, such universal success as did M. Rostand. But though he became more gradually, if less widely, known, he was, in a way, more stimulating and inspiring thereby. M. Rostand became famous at one stroke. With Hauptmann each new play was a successive emotion and excitement. Every new play was a new revelation of the soul of the artist; it raised, for one and another while, those clouds which keep from the average soul that intellectual horizon which it longs for, that emotional sunlight which puts everything into the vivid reality, and makes even common things for the time being lovely.

44

GERHARDT HAUPTMANN

Hence the thrill with which one first read the words—

" Open the window. Let in Light and God! " To those who had followed Hauptmann play after play, they had the added demonstration of actual experience.

It was in 1889 that " Vor Sonnenaufgang " was given by the Freie Bühne. The performance was made a battlefield between the old school and the new. The inordinate excitement of that war, of the war of which that was a campaign, has now died down. I remember it, and would wonder at myself for having been so stirred by it, did I not remember also how sincere the emotion was. " Horrible things were witnessed " in that play; " A picture of hell itself would have paled by the side of it; Zola and Tolstoi would have had to confess ' He can do better than we.' " Such were the expressions of Spielhagen some time afterward, who held the battlefield to have been a Waterloo for the new school.

When we look back it seems natural enough. Hauptmann was of a very sensitive, artistic disposition. He had not found his real power in his efforts at sculpture, nor in his studies in zoölogy, nor in his essays at poetry. It was very natural that, unless he had been strongly impelled in some very different direction, he should have followed the influences of the moment. And given so much, it was not remarkable that he should have gone ahead of the advance.

When one reads Hauptmann's early plays, " Vor Sonnenaufgang," " Das Friedensfest," " Einsame Menschen," one thinks, necessarily almost, of Tolstoi, Zola, Ibsen. They give us pretty consistent realism in form and matter. The last is by far the best, but if Hauptmann had done no better, he would hardly remain in the minds of those who have no especial turn for German literature. Looking back to the play, I recall most readily the figure of Anna Mahr. It is almost worth while to re-read the play to vivify that strong and delicate figure, typical of so much of the life of her time and of ours, at once suggestive and tragic. And yet even as a figure—entirely aside from the play—Anna Mahr is not the dramatic figure that will flash to mind in Magda. And whether she be or not, the play itself is certainly not greater than " Mutter Erde." So far at least Hauptmann had not shown himself greater than Sudermann or Max Halbe. He went on, however, and did more.

He remained a realist, even a naturalist. But there is not much reminiscence of the great leaders in the plays that immediately followed. Hauptmann now strikes out more for himself. In " Die

Weber " he goes as far as one can readily imagine
the stage can go. The play is written of a weavers'
strike. It is not, however, a play that takes a
weavers' strike for a background, or a setting,
or a situation in which a hero, or heroine, other
characters shall be presented. The play takes
the strike itself for its subject. There is no hero
and no heroine; characters there are, but only
because there must be people on the stage to have
any play at all. The same people do not hold
our interest; quite a new set of people appear in
the third act, and we hardly hear of the old ones.
The strike, however, is before us throughout; the
strike is the only character of importance; men
and women appear and disappear only that the
strike may be presented to us. An extraordinary
conception, and one subversive of the common
ideas of the stage, but logical enough realism.
Hauptmann read about the strike in a pamphlet,
and proceeded to put it on the stage. The wonder
is that he could make it seem dramatic and powerful. This wonder, however, he was able to accomplish.

Still realistic, but this time with a truly artistic
contempt for logic, Hauptmann next produced a
play about a beaver-skin. You may see it on the
German stage to-day: " Devilish funny, but no
drama and no art," I am told by a wholly com-

petent authority. I am sorry to say that of it I can read only about one word in four, which gives me but a fragmentary idea of what it presents. I must pass it by; I have enjoyed Hauptmann greatly without it.

This play, however, and another, " College Crampton," I learn from the conscientious biographer of Hauptmann, were suggested in spirit by Molière. And without as a rule going into the question of influences and sources and so on, it is curious to note for the moment the different forms in which this realist presents himself to us, or, rather, presents his view of the world. Realism, in Zola's phrase, consists of the facts of life seen through a temperament. Hauptmann's temperament would seem to be that of the chameleon; he is a modern Proteus, and sounds his horn from under many disguises. In his first play he is like Tolstoi, in his second like Zola, in his third like Ibsen. In his fourth we see through the eyes of Dr. Zimmermann the pamphleteer. In the fifth it is Molière. Certainly (if Zola be right) it is a curious thing that the man will not see through his own temperament.

Still it is to be remarked that another man, and he also the greatest artist in letters of his nation of his day, did just the same thing. Robert Louis Stevenson was a very different man from

Hauptmann, and had a very different view of the world. But he was like him in that, whatever his temperament, his artistic and poetic nature was always curiously trying and testing new and particular methods and ways of doing what he wished to do,—" Dr. Jeykll and Mr. Hyde," " Prince Otto," " Treasure Island," " Will o' the Mill," " The Black Arrow," he is as romantic as Hauptmann is realistic. We might recognise all those books as by the same man, but in them, as in Hauptmann's first plays, we see the man using the different forms, the modes of expression that we are familiar with elsewhere. It is not that an original genius must of necessity invent an original form; that is far from the truth. But that an original genius should adopt such varying specialities of form, each of which seems characteristic of something in itself, that does seem singular. It would seem to be one of the curious things in the psychology of the artist that the most exquisite natures often have this mimetic character. Perhaps it is because they are the most sensitive; Whistler was a man rather like that.

In all these things, however, Hauptmann was a realist, by which I mean that he was absorbed and interested in the facts of life, and thought it well to present them in much the same way that

he saw them. The romanticist does not do that:
he commonly presents his view of life in forms
that he has not seen. M. Rostand has something to
say; he likes to present it in forms very different
from the forms he sees around him. A fanciful
anywhere " if the costumes are pretty," the mar-
vellous East of the Crusades, the bare but glowing
hills of Galilee, Old Paris, Schönbrunn and the
field of Wagram,—these places and the people
appertaining to them are interesting to him.
They recur to his mind, take form and combina-
tion there, gain a significance from his theory of
life, from their relation to it, and when they develop into a finished play they are found to present a fact or facts, a meaning, a lesson, even, for
such as wish to be taught, but all in the glowing,
glorious, poetic, imaginative, beautiful figures
that the poet loved.

It is not so with Hauptmann. His ideas are
different from those of M. Rostand for one thing.
M. Rostand stands aloof and generalises. But
Hauptmann is near enough to be intensely moved
by great wrongs and great struggles for redress.
He is so near the particular thing that he becomes
absorbed in it. Why should a man who wants to
present the cruelty and crime involved in the failure of a great strike, why should he write about
the Sacred Mount and the belly and the members?

True, Shakespeare took that way to say what he wished to say, but then Shakespeare can hardly have felt about current life as Hauptmann did. He was a larger man and had larger views, but certainly he controlled very well any great sympathy he might have had for some of his more limited brothers and sisters.

Hauptmann went in for it seriously. He would show the world as it was. And whether he took the method of Ibsen or of Molière, he was always there himself with his sympathy, his ideas, and his poetry.

For that he was a poet appeared in what came next. I like " Hanneles Himmelfahrt " best of all Hauptmann's work, and I am quite sure that it is the most characteristic thing he has done. I mean to re-read it at this moment. Or, rather, I would, except that here it is better to write from one's recollection than with one's eye on the text. The drama ought to make, to have made, an impression on one; if it does not it fails, and by as much as the impression is not lasting, by so much has the drama failed of its possibilities.

From the midst, then, of a time years back, a time full of other work and other interests, a time separated from Now by all sorts of differences, appears the figure of Hannele cowering in her miserable little bed, and of the Angel of Death

looming up affectionately before the high stove;
and again of the little girl all aglow with interest
and excitement, and the good and kind tailor,
who has brought her the white dress and crystal
slippers; and again of the appearance of the
stranger, the worker, the physician, him of the
robe without a stain who comes to guide her
whither she is to go.

Well, and what of it all? I can imagine some
disagreeable person saying. Frankly, reader, I
do not quite know. Those figures were very
beautiful to me once—if I read the play again
they would be beautiful once more.

But beyond that they have their significance.
I cannot now remember just what they did signify
to me once, nor can I say that in Hauptmann's
mind they ever signified such and such thoughts.
That would give something of a false idea. Hauptmann, himself a thorough-paced realist so far,
now presents an object different from anything
that had come from his hand. It is now realistic
psychology, as we may say, that is the main thing.
Here is the country almshouse and the wretched
creatures in it; here is a poor, abused little girl
who is brought there to die. The play follows
her last hours and presents her feverish and fan-
tastic thought. All that follows—the figure of
her dead mother, the three angels, the sudden

changes, the great angel with dark garments and
dark wings, the village tailor, the stranger—is but
the creation of the fading power of the childish
soul, mingled curiously with the realities of the
Deaconess, Pastor Gottwald, and the poor creatures of the almshouse. That, as a subject for
a " dream poem," was Hauptmann's interest, I
suppose, and not such and such ideas signified
thereby.

Still the figure and the passing dream bring
ideas and moods, and bring, too, moments of
serenity to the soul, even when somewhat choked
with the materialities of ashes or sugar plums.

In this play Hauptmann is more himself than
ever before or since. Heretofore he had tried
different forms, henceforward he tries more; there
seems no end to his power of varying the mask
of form. But everything else that he wrote could
be put alongside of something else. The early
plays have easy analogues; even " Die Weber "
was preceded by Verhaeren's " The Dawn," which
is not unlike it. The later plays, too, are in general not unlike others. " Die versunkene Glocke "
is one of a number of Märchendramen, " Florian
Geyer " is a historic play, in form at least much
what Wildendruch might have written; in " Fuhrmann Henschel " he was said at once to have " returned " to something that his admirers approved.

But "Hanneles Himmelfahrt," the Traum-
dichtung, resembles nothing else that I can think
of. It has all the rest of Hauptmann,—the realism, the psychology, that we have seen,—joined
to the romance and the poetry that were to have
freer play in years to come. In motive it is a
little like Maeterlinck's "Mort de Tintagiles,"
and creates something of the same effect. But
that is a very different kind of work, and entirely
lacks the vitality which is one of the virtues of
" Hannele."

Like most of the previous plays, " Hannele "
created a considerable stir, this time on religious
grounds as well as those of art. Hauptmann
went on calmly, and instead of trying to do again
anything he had done well once, he wrote a historical drama, " Florian Geyer," into which he
put his whole energy, only to meet with a failure.
It was followed by " Die versunkene Glocke," the
play which made Hauptmann really famous, by
which he is generally known.

And yet the play is, in a way, not representative. If you read only " A Tale of Two Cities "
you might perhaps wonder that Dickens is often
thought of as a humourist. If you read only
" Die versunkene Glocke " you will wonder, perhaps, why Hauptmann should be thought of as
a realist. For it is a romantic, fairy play in

poetry, very different certainly from the plays
which had gone before, and different too from
those that followed. It is without much doubt
the greatest piece of work of its author, but it is
work in a very different direction from that in
which we are accustomed to look for him. It
was first acted in 1896, and will doubtless be remembered by many either at the Irving Place
Theatre or as given by Mr. Sothern.

The play begins at once. Up the mountain,
into the old, undisturbed world of romance, comes
the artist, broken-hearted at the failure of his
work for men. He had tried, perhaps, to do too
much, and has met failure.

It is very beautiful, certainly, this world of
romance. It was beautiful on the stage, and it
is still beautiful in the play, for one of the charms
with which literature compensates for its lack of
vivid visual impressions is that it lasts. It is
like the walls of Camelot, which were not built at
all and are therefore built for ever. So we can
go at will to that upland mountain-meadow, with
its violets and primroses, and the bees that sip
gold from the crocuses, and the pines that rustle
round about. There the Nickelmann lives, or there
he appears in the spring from his home deep down
underneath the hills. He is hoary and covered
with moss and weeds. There, too, lives the wood-

scrattle, a coarse and licentious creature who
strangely smokes a pipe. There, also, are dwarfs
and elves. There is Rautendelein, half human, it
would seem, and half a bit of nature. She plays
with the bee and teases the Nickelmann and dances
with the elves, if she chooses, and jeers at the
wood-scrattle and his goatish legs. She has a
grandmother, too, a wise woman, who leads rather a
surly existence among these simple folk and feeds
the little Trolls with milk. The German forest
is certainly a fine place, and I have always loved
it, from early readings in Grimm down; we have
no such creatures in our forests. And I have
forgotten the dwarfs who are there, too; and all
is up on the mountain-side, far above the abodes
of men. Nature has withdrawn to herself before
the march of civilisation. What elements of
humanity there are are merely animal, unless we
except the natural knowledge of the Wittich.

So much the play certainly has developed and
carried out with description and picture; so much
for every one, whether more or not. Nature and
art the play presents, and like any fine big piece
of work, it is full of all sorts of things that reward
a reader who may come again and again, as one
may climb a mountain again and again, and
always find something new on the way, although
there is always the same view from the top. When

Keats wrote " Endymion " he very sensibly noticed
that it was one of the things that people liked,
to have enough in a poem to be able to pick and
choose, to find always some new charm or something perhaps that had once charmed and then
slipped from mind. In this forest region we can
walk often, always finding something to notice,
something quaint, beautiful, stimulating.

Into this world of nature wanders Heinrich, the
artist. He had almost finished a great and beautiful work and has been bitterly disappointed by
failure at the final moment. He gains by chance
a glimpse of Nature in her secret beauty and
charm. Before he is brought back to the valley
by his friends who have come to look for him, he
sees Rautendelein.

And here, with the very beginning of the action
of the play, comes an element into the play that
is not so simply handled—namely, that which is
loosely called the symbolism of the play. It would
seem that in this play of the Artist and Nature
and the World of Men, there must be some hidden
meaning. It arouses our curiosity,—a little, I
am afraid, like a cryptograph,—we want to know
what it all means.

The artist who has endured a bitter failure has
a glimpse of the secrets of nature, and though
borne down to his home on lower levels, it is by

one of the spirits of nature that he is cured. He
leaves his home, and with the fresh, natural being
he has learned to know he goes up the mountain,
back to nature once more. He finds his strength
increased tenfold. But the power of humanity
is too strong; his dead wife draws him down from
his retreat. And as for his beautiful spirit of
nature, half human as she seems, the power of
nature is too much for her; she is drawn down
among the founts at the foundations of the earth.
This is the essential story of the " Versunkene
Glocke " shorn of its colour, and beauty, and body.
What would Hauptmann signify by it?

If it were pretty obvious that he wished to signify something of importance, I should think that
one ought to know what it is. But as the significance is clearly something not, on the face of it,
obvious—for the author's countrymen have presented quite a number of different explanations
of it—I am content to read the play as a play
rather than a conundrum.

So then it may be asked: Is the figure of Heinrich without significance? And, if so, why should
any dramatic poem have significance? What does
Rudel stand for? Cyrano? L'Aiglon? If these
figures are significant, why not Heinrich? Surely
it is an eccentric outcome to one's speculation that
presents M. Rostand as the dramatist of ideas and

Hauptmann the dramatist of legendary romance alone.

The play certainly offers us dramatic situations. Let us take one at random. The Pastor has come to persuade Heinrich to leave the mountain where he is living joyfully and doing great work and to return to his home. The artist is flushed with success; the visitor is by no means disconcerted at what he sees around him. " Now God be thanked!" says he. " You are the same old friend.

Heinrich. I am the same—and yet another, too. Open the window. Let in Light and God.

Pastor. A noble saying.

Heinrich. I know none better.

Pastor. I know of better—still that one is good."

Here, certainly, in these few words between the Artist who has abandoned his place among men and gone to the heart of nature, and the Priest who has gone to put before him the claim of a power higher than nature, here there certainly is significance, such as any one can see, such as is almost explicit in words and characters. But further there cannot be any symbolic significance found for it which equals the real and fundamental significance of the words and situation. Take the simplest kind of symbolic significance—let us

say, there are Art and Religion. Surely any such
abstraction as that is absolutely empty of meaning when we compare it with the creation of the
Artist and the Man of God. We have the meaning
when we merely create in our minds Heinrich, the
Bell-caster, who is at work among the mountains,
and the Pastor of his earlier days, who seeks to
bring him back to his home. I do not mean to go
into it as a question of Realist or Ideal Philosophy,
but merely to speak of it as a matter of the drama.
And here, we may say without the slightest doubt,
that whatever abstract idea may be implied in
words and situation, it can add little to the real
meaning of them. Compared with the intellectual
and emotional powers which could create the situation and words, any further thinking which
could be tacked to them by allegory, will seem
feeble in the extreme. " To one reader, ' Die
versunkene Glocke,' conveys a certain impression;
to another an entirely different significance may
be suggested. Both may be right." On the other
hand both may be, and probably are, wrong, if
" significance " means explanation of the meaning,
for the real appeal of the drama is not in any
significance or meaning, but in its figures and its
situations and what they are. Heinrich leaves his
wife and children and goes up the mountain with
Rautendelein. Why say that it typifies anything

more than Rip Van Winkle, who did much the
same thing, except that his elfish beings were
stout little Dutchmen instead of charming young
women. The situation is certainly one which
makes a wide appeal to all sorts of lurking in-
stincts of the heart. Man is not yet so absolutely
civilised that such a rush to freedom does not at
times seem an escape from bothers and monotonies
which he would often be without. But is it any
real addition to the impression to say that Art
finds Domesticity irksome and seeks the freedom
of Nature? I fancy not. That is a very simple
piece of generalisation and from a very small number of examples, but however that may be, it is
not as a generalisation that the thing will interest
us. If we wanted a generalisation we should go to
the moralist, who would give us the facts with the
proper inductions and deductions. What we want
is something for the imagination, something that
we can sympathise with, something that will have
more effect upon the fierce fret and grind of darker
moments than any abstraction has yet been found
to have. And that we get from the figure itself,
not from any meaning which it symbolises.

No—I think we shall gain little by inquiring as
to the symbolism of " Die versunkene Glocke."
If it were real symbolism it would be another
thing. In real symbolism—as that of William

Blake—the poet, or the painter, has some meaning that he conveys by absolute symbols, which, unless we know their meaning, will give us no more hint of it, than a page of Plato would give a newborn child.   Thus, in Blake's illustrations to the book of Job, we observe the moon to be sometimes in one corner of the picture, sometimes in the other. That conveys a difference of meaning.   I forget what it is—I thought it of interest at the time I knew it—but the point is that unless you know that difference of meaning, you will miss the idea of the picture.   That is real symbolism.   If you do not know the key to Blake, it is impossible (unless you make one) to know what his pictures are about.

With Hauptmann, as with most artists with whom the question is raised, the matter is different. With them we generally have, not almost arbitrary symbols, but typical figures.   The difference is very clear.   The cross is a symbol; the fish used to be a symbol.   But nobody could have guessed what they were symbols of who did not know the associations which gave them meaning.   On the other hand, the Good Samaritan is no symbol; as soon as any one knows who and what he was his significance is plain and needs no explanation.   In like manner Heinrich is doubtless a typical figure, just as Faust is, or Manfred, or Brand.   But

whatever he is a type of, he himself is, so that one
who knows him, and who feels his passion and his
action, has what the poet meant to present, and
more important, has it in the form in which the
poet meant to present it. A man may prefer to
translate the poet's language into his own, but
that will be because he does not understand poetry,
or does not like it. It may be a curious intellectual
exercise to speculate farther, but unless there is
very good ground for supposing that the poet
himself went farther, we shall probably miss what
he meant to express in aiming at what he did not
think of.

Of the succeeding plays of Hauptmann, I do
not propose to speak. Those who thought of
" Die versunkene Glocke " as the beginning of a
new epoch, received a shock in " Fuhrmann Henschel." " Die versunkene Glocke " was presented
toward the end of 1896; a year afterwards appeared " Cyrano de Bergerac," and it appeared
that a great romantic awakening was beginning.
It seems almost cynical for Hauptmann at such
a period to be considering the situation of a Sile-
sian carter, who having promised his dead wife not
to marry, now wished to marry the maid of the
house. The play was psychological. Now psychology has its romance, but " Fuhrmann Henschel " did not carry on the torch uplifted in " Die

versunkene Glocke." Nor did "Schluck und
Jau." This was a thoroughly characteristic piece
of work; at a time when the world thought it knew
what Hauptmann could do, he proceeded to do
something quite beyond anybody's reckoning.
Few, however, cared for the "Shakespearean"
farce, nor am I among the number. "Michael
Kramer" and "Der rote Hahn" were not such sur-
prises, but they were not much more successful.
Indeed the period of these plays was generally
regarded as a period of artistic decadence on the
part of the poet: his right hand seemed to have
lost its cunning. His admirers became perplexed,
or irritated, or despondent.

From this feeling they were raised by the production of "Der arme Heinrich." Here was a
play which appeared at once to be a very fine
thing. It was, however, curious that it should
have been by Hauptmann. For Hauptmann is
essentially an individualist: in his work he tries
not to do something of a recognised or regular
kind in order, but to express himself in his own
way. And the people in his plays are individual-
ists, too. Anna Mahr in "Einsame Menschen" or
Heinrich the Bell-founder; they live for self-realisation. "Der arme Heinrich" offers a contrast.
The play is founded on the poem of Hartmann von
Aue; the story tells how Heinrich, lord of Aue, a

brilliant and splendid knight, distinguished by the
king and famous for his exploits in the Crusades,
chief paladin of the Holy Roman Empire, at the
very height of his glory and the vigour of his life
and joy in the world, was suddenly struck with
leprosy. Instead of being the most wonderful of
those remarkable combinations of imagination and
action which the mediæval chivalry holds out to us,
he became simply an outcast, an object of loath-
ing, one who had to live in some squalid place by
himself, and who had to strike continually on a
wooden clapper that people might know that he
was near and avoid him.

That is a fine subject for the individualist; a
leper has to live his own life partly because no one
else wants to live any part of it for him, and partly
because no one else will let him share a life in common. In the beginning of the play Heinrich is
among those who are devoted to him, a liegeman
of the house of Aue, an old retainer, a farm ten-
ant and his wife. They are not only his followers,
but they love him, before they know his secret.
Then his clapper sends a shiver through them.

There is therefore an interest, perhaps unpoetic,
in the lord and leper. Why does Hauptmann,
whose heroes seemed ready to stand out for themselves against God and man, who lived their own
lives and died their own deaths, why does he now

present to us the figure of one who, in his pride, is guilty of insolence to God and is struck down by the powers he has scorned into a terrible irony of the state to which he aspired? And why, as a sequel to Heinrich the Bell-founder, does he elect to present a man, who, in seeking the highest, falls to the lowest, and must be rescued from the most awful depths by the unselfish devotion of a girl who, so far from wishing to live for herself, desires rather to die for him?

The later plays of Hauptmann have not sustained the hopes raised by " Der arme Heinrich." " Rose Bernd " was not so unsuccessful in Germany, but has never been widely known. And of the others, " Und Pippa Tanzt " is almost the only one that has been heard of outside of Germany, and in Germany they have given rise to the idea of " a second decadence " on the part of the poet. Not long since he published a novel, " Emmanuel Quint," and it was thought that perhaps he was going to turn from the drama to fiction, as Sudermann had turned from fiction to the stage. But " Die Ratten " last winter seemed to do away with that idea and to create no other.

The three finest things of Hauptmann are still " Hannele " and " Der arme Heinrich " on the one hand, and " Die versunkene Glocke " on the other. These plays make a strange contrast. They present to us two conceptions which are consistent only as many of the strange antinomies of life are consistent, in being both true at once, we cannot well say how. The two strains of revolt and resignation; one in the figure of the artist maintaining himself stiffly through the darkness till daybreak, and the other poor humanity (prince like beggar girl) which bows the head and finds happiness in submission.

These three plays, I find, are almost the only ones of Hauptmann that I care much to look over, that abide in my mind. Perhaps it is because I am growing more romantic with the added years (contrary to the usual notion that youth is the time for romance) and do not care so much for the sanded arena of the world as in the period of youth. Perhaps, also, I should not have liked " Der arme Heinrich " twenty years ago as well as the story of Heinrich the Bell-founder. But now, having paid my money (in various ways), I rather like to take my choice.

SUDERMANN

THERE used to be, in Germany at least, quite a general critical opinion which placed Sudermann as a dramatist somewhere between Hauptmann and Wildenbruch. Hauptmann was the delight of the advanced guard and Wildenbruch was the favourite of the conservatives; Sudermann seemed to be somewhere between the two. As far as one could learn, however, he was not admired by advanced guard and conservative alike, but on the other hand was condemned at least by the ultras of each party. One side called him a compromiser and conventionalist, and the other said that he merely used old technique for exploiting sensational claptrap in the way of so-called ideas. The more advanced said that his dialogue was written for schoolgirls, the conservatives said that his material was light-headed extravagance. He was, I believe, in Germany the representative of " Realismus," while Hauptmann's particular lay was " Naturalismus," and Wildenbruch's I don't know just what.

For myself I am inclined to like this middle po-

HERMANN SUDERMANN

sition and to think of his plays in the words applied to that unknown dramatist whose works were
caviare to the general (not that Sudermann's
are), namely, that it is " an excellent play, well
digested in the scenes, set down with as much
modesty as cunning." His method is, compara-
tively speaking, as wholesome as sweet, and by
very much more handsome than fine. In other
words, while Sudermann's plays have not the brilliancy and exhilaration of some of the dramatists
of our day, in form at least, and dialogue, they
are well put together and written. But with such
matters it would be impertinent for me to meddle,
for one would hardly expect one who did not follow German literature pretty closely to have an
opinion on these things.

Nor are they much in my line, although there
is or may be a good deal of interest in them. If
one have read more or less of the literature of the
last twenty-five years in the various parts of the
world, and seen pictures, and heard music, and
gone to the theatre, there is fascination in these
considerations of schools and tendencies and influences, past, present, and future. There is something inspiring in the largeness of it. And certainly, too, there is a sort of lyric fervour in
Hauptmann which one may feel the lack of in
Sudermann. And in Wildenbruch there is doubt-

less something, too (only I can never quite get at it), which brings out by contrast the qualities of Sudermann. And it must be inspiring to read " Sturmgeselle Sokrates " and to speculate on the future of the German drama.

But all that, in itself, seems to me to neglect so much. Sudermann is so intent on personality that when I see a play of his or read one (which is much more often), all talk of influence or estimates falls into the background, while my sympathies and emotions are more wrung, I believe, than by any of the others, and always have been. Not that it is everything to have one's sympathies and emotions wrung,—it does not necessarily mean the highest art,—but it surely is something, and a something that does not leave one free to consider questions of criticism. Nor can it be to me alone that the plays of Sudermann make a very personal appeal. Bernard Shaw can undoubtedly show us hollow places in our modern life so that we recognise the truth with a quick thrill of pleasure. But however things ought to be, there are some things that thrill us now. And if Sudermann cannot, or does not, see just what life should be, he certainly can give us sudden realisations of what life actually is; can touch us to the quick by his poignant moments of life as we realise it, moments in which we cease for the time from being so-

cial figures and relapse into individualism. M. Rostand takes us as individuals and touches us by an
appreciation of select moods, of our higher and
better moods; he presents to us, in his curiously
pessimistic way, moments of personality, ideals of
possibility, of standing rigidly in one's own self
while the world melts and crumbles away below.
But if Sudermann cannot or does not have much
to say about the ideal, he certainly can give us
keen feelings of the way our personality comes
in contact with those personalities next to us, who
are with us day by day, enveloped, save for one
time and another, in the impenetrable reserve that
keeps us commonly each to ourself.

Sudermann's motives are always, in his most
characteristic plays at least, combinations of those
great conflicts, or at least antagonisms or discords
of life, that every one, here in America to some degree, as well as in Germany, finds among the conditions with which he must take account. Home
and the outside world, the old generation and the
new, conventionalism and individualism, personality and society, faith and new ideas, art and
everyday life—who is there to-day who has not
some personal experience of such things as these?
Strife or conflict may be too stern a name for
them in ordinary life; but surely they make disharmonies, incongruities, and often worse. Do

they make up more of our life to-day than they
did of the life in other times? I cannot say, but
certainly they make much. And it is an evidence
that Sudermann sees life truly, in its larger lines,
that, in his stronger plays, they are rarely miss-
ing.

Not that these motives are always dragged into
his dramas, but it would seem as if these ideas, being often in his mind, continually influenced his
choice of subject or the moulding of his material.
" Die Ehre," his first play, has much the same
subject as Wildenbruch's " Die Haubenlerche ":
each concerns the relations of a rich family to a
poor family among its dependents; each shows the
rich offering benefits for a return in flesh and
blood and honour. There are strong situations
in each play and both were successful on the stage.
But Wildenbruch's play is thin and conventional
compared to Sudermann's, on account of the con-
flicting motives in " Die Ehre " to which one easily
finds an answer in one's own life. Robert, who
has been ten years in India, accustomed to a
larger, more modern life, comes back to a re-
stricted, old-fashioned, very lower middle-class
family; Alma, who has stayed at home, has been
continually escaping from the annoyances of
parental control to the temptations of the free,
half-bohemian circle to which she finds her way,

It is all the same sort of thing that we may easily
see around us; it does not take particularly striking forms as we see it, but it would if a dramatist
should deal with it. Robert comes back from the
freedom of his independent life to the pettiness
of his old father and mother; so do hundreds of
boys and girls come back from college, say, to
the farm. Alma, who chafes under the restric-
tions of the elder generation, wishes to seek the
glittering show of pleasure in her own way; and
we have examples of that, too, from the farm to
the city, or from the house to the street. It is
no great exhibition of genius to have noted so
much, but it is, I think, a piece of genius to con-
ceive an action that shall be a focus for half a
dozen such motives, to carry it on by characters
that shall continually represent them to us, and
to express them and comment on them by con-
tinual epigram or chance remark that strike us
surely and often remain in the mind.

Just what the action is seems to me of lesser
importance, if only it be interesting. " Die
Ehre " was a successful play, and the critics, as
a whole, paid very little attention to what I have
been speaking of. Thus Bulthaupt, who is representative enough, criticises the play severely
because of Graf Trast's disquisitions on Honour.
Now that turns the play into what is hideously

called a problem-play. And further, it makes the play something that we, over here, cannot easily get hold of, for our ideas on Honour are different in many respects from those current in Germany, and though we may understand their feeling well enough, and Sudermann's criticisms of it, yet it can hardly be a matter which we shall feel very keenly. Most Americans, I fancy, would agree with Graf Trast—he is meant to be a man who had seen the world—in his view that Honour differs with different people, being one thing in one nation or class and something else in another, and that if conventional honour were dispensed with in favour of duty, the world would be quite as well off.

But is this sort of speculation the play? Is a play the resolution (however good) of such a problem? Hardly; here is a play of men and women and the tides of life. Surely such things are more interesting than questions and problems, certainly more widespread.

Whether they are or not, this may be said: the same discords or disharmonies of life that one observes in " Die Ehre " are to be seen in " Sodom's Ende." It is true that this play ostensibly differs from the former; that play offers us, according to the critics, a criticism of current conceptions of honour, and this, they tell

us, is a criticism of some current conceptions of
artistic life.

But if one do not think of such things, one finds
that here too we have personalities and the currents of life of our time. Here is the cramped
home of the ruined proprietor turned milk-in-
spector, and the phosphorescent rottenness of his
son Willy, a notable figure in the great (Berlin)
world of art and ideas. Here are the simple conceptions of the old people and the younger but
decadent world of the critics, and those who catch
up their words. Here is the dim but deeply
rooted conception of duty and the half-acknow-
ledged sophistries of those who think their own
thoughts and live their own lives. Perhaps the
play is not so broad as " Die Ehre," but it is
stronger in its action, for each play of course
has some action which finds its course in the inter-
action of the forces of the world which it por-
trays. Its chief figure is more striking than
Robert in " Die Ehre." Willy Janikow is not so
much a character as a personality. The artist of
promise, son of parents whose life is now of the
hardest, the man who has come to success in a
world where he cannot keep his head, loved by
so many and such a hard master to himself, I
remember him well sitting in the fading daylight
in his father's house, which he is about to leave,

murmuring " Reinheit, Reinheit." I remember
him well as he gathers himself together in his
studio, but too late, with the cry of " Arbeit!"
just as the curtain falls. Somewhat conventional
that is, without a doubt; Sudermann uses conventional modes of expression in a way Hauptmann
would never do, and that seems to take away from
his power with many. But I do not think that
it stands in the way of effect; it does not seem to
stand in the way of sincerity.

But it is in " Heimat " that all these motives
have freest play. As it is given in English, the
play is always called " Magda," and that is something of a mistake. And the character of Magda
has attracted the greatest actresses of our day,—
Bernhardt, Duse, Mrs. Campbell, Mrs. Fiske,—
and that, though not a mistake, is something that
rather veils the true nature of the play. Each
of those powerful actresses was so intent on her
rendering of the principal woman in the play that
she gave no great pains to the presentation of the
play as a whole—perhaps, indeed, did not understand it.

Curiously enough, a theatrical critic of great
ability showed not long ago how one may readily
see one thing so well that he sees others very ill
or not at all. " In the discussions the play first
called down upon us," he remarked on seeing Mrs.

Fiske as Magda, " it was assumed that it dealt
with the question of parental authority. . . . It
was also assumed that it dealt with the problem
of the new woman. . . . I wish to suggest that
this view is very short-sighted. Beneath the
transitory details of the play it seems to me that
there is a motive which is eternal." Certainly
there is, and the only thing noteworthy in this
remark is that it is a suggestion resulting from
" a growing suspicion." While seeing Duse and
Bernhardt and Mrs. Fiske, the suspicion grew
upon his mind that this play was not the exploitation of a current " problem," but that it had a
motive of eternal interest. At first he missed the
real things in the play. That may have been
because he was a theatrical critic, and naturally
most interested in the acting. But Magda is not
the only character in the play; she is the most
brilliant, but probably the pastor, Heffterdingt,
was the author's chief effort. And the play is
not specifically about the new woman and parental
authority. It presents to us, as " Die Ehre "
does, the contrast between the provincial life and
the big world. It shows us, as " Sodom's Ende "
does, the conflict between the quiet virtues of home
and the brilliant temptations of art. It shows us,
as " Es lebe das Leben " does, the difference between fulfilling one's own personality and follow-

ing the normal and narrow ideas of duty. Nor
is that all; it does show us paternal authority,
but that is only the German form taken by the
constant difference between the older generation
and the newer. It does show us the new woman,
but that is only a current form of the difference
between new ideas and conservatism or conventionalism, as you may choose to call it. In one
situation as a focus are all these lines of life. Nor
is it in the situation only—the return of the
brilliant prodigal daughter—that these motives
are implicit. They are everywhere indicated in
the lines of the characters.

"Modern ideas," says the old soldier, "oh,
pshaw! I know them. But come into the quiet
homes where are bred brave soldiers and virtuous
wives. There you'll hear no talk about heredity,
no arguments about individuality, no scandalous
gossip. There modern ideas have no foothold, for
it is there that the life and the strength of the
Fatherland abide. Look at this home! There is
no luxury,—hardly even what you call good taste,
—faded rugs, birchen chairs, old pictures; and
yet, when you see the beams of the western sun
pour through the white curtains, and lie with such
a loving touch on the old room, does not something
say to you, ' Here dwells true happiness? ' "

And when Magda looks about her, " Every-

thing's just the same," says she. " Not a speck of
dust has moved." And her mother answers, solic-
itously, " I hope that you won't find any specks
of dust."

And when Magda speaks to her sister, " Come
here—close—tell me the truth—has it never entered your mind to cast this whole network of pre-
caution and respect away from you, and to go
with the man you love out and away—anywhere—
it doesn't matter much—and as you lie quietly on
his breast, to hurl back a scornful laugh at the
whole world which has sunk behind you? "

" No, Magda," says Marie, " I never feel so."

One might copy out pages of quotations, so
remarkable is the way in which the action of character upon character brings out motives that are
vital. I will confess that I hardly know whether
all this is precisely what one would call dramatic.
But that is something that must be put aside for
the moment.

These things should touch people deeply. They
are not merely interesting problems. Few of us
ever consider the problem of the new woman or
of parental authority with the idea of finding any
answer to it. But here is a home with good things
and stupid things and silly things, doubtless, as
many other homes have, and to it comes this glorious outcast who has not been feeding on swine's

husks, but has reached fame and acquired fortune and wealth and an immense retinue. In just that form we shall probably never know that motive, but every man whose wife and daughters are constantly in the world of society, and every woman whose husband spends his evenings at the club, and whose boy goes out on the streets, will be able to feel it. And so it is with the rest. As problems, we have no earthly concern with them. In the special forms which they take in Sudermann's plays we have not much to do with them, and often nothing at all, but essentially we know them and can respond to them.

And that the drama can present them is evident from these plays. That they are essentially dramatic material is another matter; it would seem as if the novel gave a wider opportunity. Sudermann is a novelist as well as a dramatist, and an exceptionally powerful one. I am not familiar with all his works, but in " Frau Sorge "—the best known of his novels on this side the water—it certainly appears that he does not use the advantage that he seems to have to present largely and fully the dominating currents of human life. Instead of so doing he seems to narrow his grasp to one powerful motive. It may be that the novelist, who must work so much by description where the dramatist can work by presentation, the

temptation is to confine oneself.   However that be
—and it is no present business of mine—the impression of Sudermann's plays is certainly that of
a world of active impulses and of human figures
living and moving therein.

It has been said, however, and perhaps it seems
obvious, that Sudermann's dramatic theme is " in
all his pieces the one single conflict in which free
personality stands with the exactions of society,"
and that " he never allows it to be doubtful that
he stands on the side of personality and that he is
a champion of its rights."   If this were the case,
it would take away the chief element of his power.
It is true that not a few dramatists in Germany
as well as elsewhere, and other men of letters as
well as dramatists, have presented of late the
rights of personality as against the pretensions
of society or some kind of society.   It has always
been a favourite motive, for artists are always
men of personality, and they are apt enough to
present its claims.   But in the present generation
the idea has been more common than before.   " To
live one's own life " has become one of the catch-
words of modern literature.   Merely among
modern German dramatists we can see the motive
in Hauptmann and in Max Halbe, in each very
tellingly presented, and we can see it also in Sudermann.   But I cannot think that it is his only dra-

matic theme, even his pre-eminent interest. It
occurs in his plays, but always in connection with
other motives. In " Die Ehre " there is no doubt
that Robert and Leonora resolve finally to rescue
themselves from a world in which they cannot
draw moral breath. Graf Trast, too, had long
ago emancipated himself from the follies under
which he had grown up, and in the play he appears
as the representative of freedom of thought
against the conventional correctness of social eti-
quette. And Sudermann here is on the side of
those who honour duty more than the arbitrary
dictum of society, as poets and sane-minded people
have been for a good while. But poor, silly little
Alma in the play is also a disciple of personality:
she also wants to live her own life as much as any
girl who went into a shop instead of a family because she wanted freedom. She wants to do as
she pleases and is bored to death with the restric-
tions which her grave brother's ideas of decency
would lay upon her. And with Alma the author
shows no more sympathy than one would naturally
have for a charming and wrong-headed young
woman.

Nor in his next play was he particularly the
champion of personality. The idea, the antith-
esis, is more important in " Sodom's Ende " than
it is in some other plays, but I should not call it

the main motive. Willy Janikow is a man of personality; but what is the society with which he is in conflict? He is not in conflict with the society which purchases his picture and prevents his painting any other; if he were, Sudermann might be " on his side and fighting for his rights." The society that he is in conflict with is the society represented by the household of his father and mother, and for his conflict with this society Sudermann does not ask the support of our sympathy.

In " Heimat " there need be no question that the idea of personality is pre-eminent; the very fact that so many great actresses have liked the part of Magda shows that clearly enough. But though Magda is the protagonist of personality in its strife against the demands of society, yet even here we cannot say that Sudermann leaves no doubt as to his own opinion. So far as the drama is concerned he has no opinion: he lets each person speak as he ought and do what he naturally would do. But the play throws its weight as much on the side of society in the person of Pastor Heffterdingt as it does on the side of personality as represented by Magda. And of whatever Sudermann be champion he allows nobility to the words of the pastor.

Magda. "And your calling—does not that bring joy enough?

Pastor. Yes, thank God, it does. But if one takes it sincerely, he cannot well live his own life in it. . . At least I cannot. One cannot exult in the vigour of his personality—that is what you mean, is it not? And then, I look into so many hearts—and one sees there too many wounds that one cannot heal, ever to be very blithe."

If Sudermann hold a brief for personality, he is a very honourable opponent and allows the champions of duty and of the rights of society a very fair chance. Even in despondency the Pastor is fine, as when he says to the woman who rejected him long before: "Yes, I have had to deaden much within my soul. My peace is as the peace of a corpse."

In fact, as one reads the play undominated by the power of some great actress, one may readily feel that Sudermann is the spokesman for a well-ordered life in common rather than for anarchy. In fact, that gave the play its name.

When we come to "Es lebe das Leben" there we need not deny that the main theme is the right of personality and there without doubt Sudermann gives us an idea of his position in the figure of Beate. And here he gives us the idea that there are natures that have some excuse for transcending social law. Still this is but one play: it was from a criticism of it that I drew the remark quoted

above, and I fancy that the influence of this particular piece was enough to colour a little the critic's recollection.

Sudermann does not carry a brief for individuality as his chief stock in trade. That is one of
the things that I like about him. Hauptmann
rather does so, but Sudermann's view of life is
much larger than one motive merely, and it is that
which gives the exhilaration to the reading of his
plays, for it is only the self-absorbed mind that
views the world as a struggle between personality
and society. One can certainly analyse the matter
so that it looks as if it were. For instance, one
antagonism that appears often in Sudermann's
plays, because it appears often in life, is the opposition between old and young, between one generation and the next. It is one of the commonest
causes of misunderstanding. And to the young
man or the young woman this matter looks as if it
were the great case of Personality vs. Society. But
it rarely is. The young man only thinks that he
wars with society because society is represented in
his mind by the precepts and powers of the elder
generation. If the children could get the upper
hand, as in " Lilliput Levee," our individualist
would find that everybody was on his side, and that
he could live his own life as much as he wished, if
it did not interfere with anybody else. The two

oppositions are based on quite different sets of fact. The antagonism of personality to society is one of the feelings absolutely necessary to the preservation of individual life, namely of life itself. The very fact that a man must feed himself first before he can be of use to society shows that there must be something of this self-assertive element. In some natures it will be more powerful, in some less; there will never be an agreement for it or against it. But the opposition between the older and the younger generation is a wholly different feeling and arises, so far as the older generation is concerned, from the conservatism that grows on a man as he grows older, from the increase in wisdom and knowledge of results, and from a lack of sympathy that comes partly from a poor memory and partly from absorption in work. Given these characteristics of mankind as it grows older and given also progress in the world, then you must have opposition of some sort between those who are just coming on the stage and those who are already there. In just the same way we could see that the motive of personality in strife with society combines easily with other motives which Sudermann observes in the world and presents in his plays. But they are not all one motive; they are many: probably more than I have noted.

What can we say is the effect of such motives,

how is it with us when we have them impressed
strongly upon us? Is it not exactly the effect of
the tragic figure? The great tragic figure affects
us as the tragedy of Rome affected Lord Byron.
" What are *our* woes and suffrance? " By comparison with great misfortunes of general appeal
and nobly born, our own griefs and miseries and
complaints against fortune calm down for a time.
But here is something different. Sudermann has
no great tragic figures—at least not in these
plays. Willy Janikow, it is true, expires at the
last moment, but we feel that it is only the necessary result of all that we have seen, nor is he ever
presented in such a way as to rouse all our sympathy. In " Heimat," Magda does not die at all:
she probably goes back to her brilliant life. It is
the old Colonel who dies, full of years, retired from
active work, as ready to go as any of us. Beate
is a tragic figure, but as such rather an exception.

Sudermann's power is not the power of tragedy
as is M. Rostand's. He makes a powerful impression, but it is stimulating rather than calming, possibly intellectual rather than emotional, on
the whole. Here is life, we say, complex, conflict-
ing in its currents, unharmonious. It takes a man
to keep afloat and pointed in the right direction.
And with that we straighten up a bit (morally)

and take a little more credit to ourselves for our
handling of such a matter. Then when a tight nip
comes we can regard the matter a little better from
the eye of reason. If it be one thing to perceive
the truth of the artist and another to be moved by
his power as a dramatist, Sudermann gives us
chiefly opportunities for the former. The latter
is not wanting in our experience of his work, any
more than it is with a good many other lesser men
who write plays. But it is in the former direction
that he is pre-eminent.

One regrets to add nothing to a discussion of the
author of " Heimat " and " Die Ehre." And yet
one cannot deny that in 1910 Sudermann is not
the figure in the literature of the world that he was
in 1905. Neither he nor his great rival Hauptmann have produced in later years anything which
has seized popular attention, even in Germany, as
did their earlier masterpieces. Sudermann's earlier
pieces are still sometimes given in England or
America. " Gluck im Winkel," for instance, was
given by the Repertory Theatre in London not
long ago, and so was " Johannisfeuer," which has
also been given in America. " Rosen " has been
translated. Yet with all Repertory Theatres and
New Theatres and Théâtres Libres we hear and
see nothing new of Sudermann. Was his fame but
a popular vogue? Do our critics, authors, and

audiences merely want some new thing? Was it
that ten years ago there was a fancy for foreign
drama, German, Spanish, Russian, anything, while
now people think they should have something " na-
tive "? Perhaps we must admit something of the
sort. Or can it be the author's fault, that his
masterpiece was but a lucky hit, that his mine was
but a pocket, that he had no real depth of knowledge of life and no real power of the drama?
Neither explanation is to be accepted, or, rather,
neither explanation quite puts the matter in the
right way. There can be little doubt, I take it,
that " Heimat " (like " Die versunkene Glocke "
somewhat later) came at just the moment in which
it would be immensely successful. Like some other
dramas which are now rather out of fashion, " The
Second Mrs. Tanqueray," for instance, or " Einsame Menschen," it was wonderfully impressive.
But those plays were but the earlier waves of a
great tide, or, to change the figure, they were like
guides who blazed the way for an army. And in
the onward march the early pioneers were gradually left behind, when they came to open country,
by the advanced guard. Sudermann, as I think of
him, holds now a hard position. He is not radical
enough to compete with the extravagants like
Bernard Shaw and those inspired by him. He does
not incline to secede from the conventional theatre

like " those authors whose interest is in extending
the scope of their art, in trying experiments, and
in satisfying their own sense of beauty and fitness."
By such bright and brilliant come-outers, he is even
classed with those impossible persons Sardou,
Scribe, and Dumas, because he can order a plot.
Those who like to have plays which are really discussions, or disquisitions, or debates in one, two,
or three acts, rather sniff at Sudermann because
he is really a master of the old-fashioned art of
handling a plot. And yet though he can make a
" well-made play," I can never think of Sudermann in common with the three just mentioned,
because he is so wholly lacking in what one would
call " theatricality." He has not the gift to
compete with those undisturbed artists like
Lavedan and other inheritors of the great dramatic
tradition. In fact he finds himself on a middle
point alone: perhaps a man of true genius must
always be there a good part of the time.

PINERO

I SHALL never, in all probability, be one to deny that Mr. Pinero is a consummate playwright. As to whether he be a great dramatist, whether his plays be literature, whether he can be said to offer to the world a " criticism of life," whether he have a message—these are points on which I can imagine some discussion, can imagine even taking part in it, but I cannot readily think of a dispute as to his craftsmanship in stage technique.

One reason for this, I am willing to admit, is that I have but a very hazy idea as to what stage technique is. Mr. Howells—who, to be sure, will not be accepted as authority by all who are learned on this point—Mr. Howells, or at least one of his characters, says in " The Story of a Play " that there is no such thing. " They talk about a knowledge of the stage," says Maxwell, " as if it were a difficult science, instead of a very simple piece of mechanism whose limitations and possibilities any one may seize at a glance. All that their knowledge of it comes to is claptrap, pure and simple. They brag of its resources, and tell you the car-

penter can do anything you want nowadays, but if
you attempt anything outside of their tradition,
they are frightened. They think that their exits
and entrances are great matters and that they
must come on with such a speech, and go off with
another; but it is not of the least importance how
they come or go, if they have something interesting to say or do." So the disappointed playwright
to his admiring wife. I have never been quite sure
whether that were Mr. Howells' own view or merely
the result of his observation of literary men who
write for the stage. I presume it may be the latter. I have a considerable interest in stage technique and would enjoy of all things having its fine
points exhibited to me by one who knew. But the
professors of that science whom I have known have
always seemed rather too general and glittering
for my academic mind to follow them. I notice of
stagecraft, however, that it is esteemed of great
importance on one side of the footlights and of
none at all on the other. In this respect it somewhat resembles the technique of painting, as Mr.
Henry Arthur Jones pointed out some time ago
in the *Nineteenth Century,* although he grounds
his opinion on very different reasons.

I know of no good treatise on the subject, and
it is, in fact, rather hard to find out just what play-
wrights and actors consider the really important

ARTHUR WING PINERO

things in the plays they present. I have noticed
one or two little things that may serve to give
something of a notion. In Miss Clara Morris's
very interesting " Life on the Stage " are one or
two bits of mention of the actor's art, of which
the following is the most suggestive:

" Mr. Daly wanted me to get across the stage,
so that I should be out of hearing distance of two
of the gentlemen . . . [There were many ex-
pedients for crossing, but none pleased Mr.
Daly, until Miss Morris suggested a smelling-
bottle] . . . He brightened quickly—clouded
over even more quickly: ' Y-e-e-s! N-o-o! at least
if it had never appeared before. But let me see—
Miss Morris, you must carry that smelling-bottle
in the preceding scene—and, yes, I'll just put in
a line in your part, making you ask some one to
hand it to you—that will nail attention to it, you
see! Then in this scene, when you leave these
people and cross the room to get your smelling-
bottle from the mantel, it will be a perfectly natural action on your part, and will give the men a
chance of explanation and warning.' "

Notice that new line in her part,—that shows
necessities and possibilities which Shakespeare did
not have to consider. Not so with the following,
which comes from an interview granted by Mr.
Stephen Phillips to a newspaper man:

" When I read ' Herod ' to [Mr. Beerbohm]
Tree, he was at the outset bored, sceptical, and
wanted nothing so much as to get through with it.
Gradually he grew more and more interested and
excited, until I came to the passage where trumpets are heard in the distance. ' Ha!' he said to
his secretary, ' you see the reason of that?' Then
he turned to me, and said : ' Have you ever been on
the stage?' He did not know I had ever been an
actor, but he divined it in that one touch." So far
Mr. Phillips in the interview: the interviewer,
R. D. B., continues, " I repeat that if it had not
been for his intimate knowledge of stagecraft, his
career as a playwright might have been cut short
right then and there, for Beerbohm Tree vows
that it was just this thing that made him accept
the young man as a coming great poet."

The last remark, if true, throws floods of light
upon our question, as well as upon Mr. Tree's
capabilities as a critic of poetry.

Of this sort of stagecraft, I fancy Mr. Pinero
must be a master, of the things belonging wholly
to the stage and necessary to make a play go; the
thousand and one little things, which, if they are
perfect, no one notices. Of course the smelling-
bottle and the trumpets are merely accidents; they
may even never have existed; but they serve to
illustrate a kind of thing that is obviously of im-

portance in any art, even though it is rarely understood, quite naturally, by a majority of those
who enjoy that art. We need no more inquire into
it than into the details of an actor's make-up.

Of a more important kind of stagecraft, too,—
which can be dimly perceived even by one so stage-
blind as a literary critic,—Mr. Pinero is a master.
The management of incidents and events so as to
bring out strongly and rightly the situations and
the characters—of this art Pinero is master as well
as of the other. I have generally considered the
best example of his skill to be the moment in " The
Profligate " when Janet Preece sees Dunstan Ren-
shaw and Lord Dangers, but perhaps something
from " Letty " will be better remembered. In the
third act of that play Mr. Letchmere (excellent
name—a corruption probably of Lechmore) and
his sister are good representatives of a fine old
crusted family who are beginning to get afraid of
themselves as being a little too representative.
Each is engaged in an affair that shows signs of
going a bit too far. Mrs. Crosbie resolves to
break hers off; there is to be a good-bye dinner
with Coppy, the future co-respondent; and she in-
vites to it her brother, who is devotedly fond of her,
begging him to stick to her that evening and see
that she does not get a chance to be run away with
by her emotions, and Coppy. So he does: he dines

with them and they have a very pleasant little
dinner, and then just as they are about to leave
the restaurant, it appears that the room is to be
taken by Mr. Mandeville, who is celebrating his
engagement to Letty. Now Letty is the young
lady with whom Mr. Letchmere has been carrying
on: it was rathe. upposed that he was not going
to see her again, now that she was about to marry
nicely " in her own class." He does, however, see
her, is asked to stay a moment for a glass of wine,
does so, arranges to run away with her, but for the
moment neglects his sister, who grasps the opportunity of being herself. That seems to me excellent. The forces that move these people are inex-
orable. Letchmere loves his sister and wants her
to be better than he, an absolutely necessary element in family feeling. He will do anything for
her to make her so,—anything except not loving
some one else's sister. So that situation is excellent. So is the next. Having persuaded Letty to
leave her awful fiancé for him, and while very happily planning with her a delightful future, he suddenly learns that the expected has happened: his
sister has flown or rather flitted. He loves his
sister, certainly, but he feels strongly that she is
in a manner disgraced. In the momentary softness
of heart, Letty recovers herself and regains terra
firma. She subsequently marries " in her own

class " and is very happy. Letchmere, I am afraid,
goes to the dogs. It takes time to tell these complicated things, but they are certainly fine pieces
of work.

Or take the second act of " Iris "—the end of
it—another masterpiece in its kind. Maldonado
has left Iris his cheque-book, which she scorns to
use, though she does not give it back. But an old
friend in trouble appeals to her; Iris wants money
to help her out and signs a cheque. She is in fact
drawn into the power of Maldonado by her very
generosity; that almost certain quality in easy,
pleasure-loving characters, sometimes the only re-
deeming quality, delivers her over to her enemy.
Surely that is very good because, though a pre-
arranged matter of detail, it is founded on human
nature.

But to get away from these matters of stagecraft or even dramatic art, matters that I must
ever handle gingerly, to another subject that now
and then comes up, namely Mr. Pinero as a man of
letters. Not long ago I saw an article on the edi-
torial page of an influential journal, which began
by saying that " another literary " artist had " un-
dertaken to reunite literature and the stage, whose
divorce has been so open and so dogmatically decreed by the melodramatists." This interested me:
I had heard talk of the divorce, although I had

not known that it was the melodramatists who had
pronounced the decree, and I was glad to hear of
the reconciliation which the article went on to
speak of as almost if not possibly quite successful.
It seemed a good deal for one single work to accomplish and I became curious about it. The literary artist in question was Mrs. Craigie or John
Oliver Hobbes (I'm sure I don't know which to call
her—or him; it's very awkward about the pro-
nouns,) and the means of reconciliation was " The
Ambassador," which subsequently appeared in
print.

I thought it rather strange that John Oliver
Hobbes should be spoken of as a leader, as one of
the very few men of letters who had had to do with
the theatre. But I found that the article drew
the line pretty sharply, for it appeared later that
" Dumas and Pinero are almost the only men who
take a high grade of literary art to the theatre."
I think this must surely have been before " Cyrano
de Bergerac," and certainly before its author had
been elected to the Academy. Still, even then it
seems to leave out a good many.

But, after all, what is a " literary play "?
What is meant by " taking literary art to the
theatre "? I don't know anything else to say, just
now, except that a literary play is one that can be
printed in a book and read with satisfaction by a

cultivated person; namely, some one like oneself. I do not see that much can be said beyond that. The fact that a man is or is not professionally con- nected with the theatre has nothing to do with it. Molière was an actor, Lessing a dramatic critic, Sheridan a manager; yet they contributed to liter- ature much more, so far as the drama is concerned, than Voltaire, Klopstock, and Addison, who were distinctly men of letters.

It may seem foolish to say that a literary play is one that is printed in a book. Still there can be no doubt that there have been plays, even " liter- ary plays," which never made a part of literature simply because they were never printed. People saw them, liked them perhaps, and forgot them: and there was an end of it. But if you print your play and can get the right people to read it, then it becomes literature, in the sense, of course, that a great deal else becomes literature. Now a good many of Mr. Pinero's plays have been printed, so here we have a topic that may readily be dis- cussed.

Mr. Pinero has written a great many plays and those of different kinds. " The Magistrate " is a delightful farce; " Sweet Lavender " is an attract- ive idyll. But Mr. Pinero's claim to consideration is not founded on farces or idylls: he is thought of especially as having written " The Second Mrs.

Tanqueray " and a number of other so-called
" problem-plays." Mr. Brander Matthews' se-
vere reprehension of M. Rostand could never be
made of Mr. Pinero. Whatever be the case about
a criticism of life, he certainly is supposed to
present problems; whether he be really influenced
or not by Ibsen or Dumas, he has some characteristics that remind us of them. What may be said
of him from this standpoint?

I do not care for the term " problem-play."
It may be a convenient expression for a play that
presents a problem, but certainly it is inelegant;
one would never speak of an adventure play, a history play, a manners play. But more funda-
mentally the term is at fault because problems as
such are not especially good subjects for plays.
Plays deal with life, and life does not consist very
largely of problems. The sociologist and the leg-
islator deal with problems, but the average man
or woman has not much to do with them save as
an interesting intellectual exercise. We are all
concerned with living, doubtless, but living does
not involve many problems, save of a very practical nature, as how to manage a small income or
how to bring up one's children or how to carry on
one's business or how to settle one's religion or
politics. Otherwise the main thing is how to carry
out an ideal which forms itself within us, not by

the resolution of problems generally, but in much more subtle ways. And even if problems were a current factor in life, a play would be a poor place for the exploiting them. A novelist may perhaps deal with problems, for he has space in which to argue them pro and con, but arguments are not very interesting to listen to.

Nor if problems were a fair test of the playwright, would Mr. Pinero fare very well. He does not, so far as I know, present himself as a problem-solver, but suppose for a moment that he did. What are his problems? " The Second Mrs. Tanqueray " presents possibly the problem, " How can a woman with a past become a woman without a past? " This problem clearly has the simple answer that she cannot do it at all, to which it may be added that no one else can either, by means observable on the stage. " The Profligate " seems to raise the novel problem, " Is it a good plan to marry a rake to reform him? " " The Notorious Mrs. Ebbsmith " has what is really more of a question, " Can a man and woman live together as intellectual companions? " which, however, is a matter that sensible people (not reformers) will not spend much time upon. So I do not feel that Mr. Pinero's problems would make him more worthy of attention than various other dramatists.

Even if he had problems, however, they would

not make plays. A good play generally gives us
some action that in its condensed dramatic form
will move us somehow, be an active factor in our
thinking and feeling; it gives us some character
often typical of an idea, or of something that we
are thinking about. By virtue of being a play it
may be able to burn these things in upon our mem-
ories. " Macbeth " gives us the wages of sin in
the form of death to the finer life and finally of the
death of the body. " Hamlet " gives us the man
of thought in the world of action. Here Mr.
Pinero might have something to give us. If he
have anything to say, being a master of stage art,
he should be able to create some figure typical of
some great element in life, some action or situation
which gathers into a focus some great experience.

I fear he does not do so. His shady ladies soon
become very shadowy in the mind. The solutions
to his " problems " are like that of Alexander over
the Gordian knot. " When Mr. Pinero essayed to
write plays such as these, dealing with the deepest
problems of life," writes a recent critic, " he chal-
lenged comparison not merely with the world of
dramatists, but with the world of thinkers." It
is going rather far to call Mr. Pinero's problems
the deepest of life or to fancy that the world of
thinkers has ever been very much concerned with
them. Mr. Pinero does not make much of them,

they do not remain with us; they hold our attention
while they are acting, but we soon lose them from
mind. This is really not so much the fault of the
thinker as of the artist. Sudermann, to take an
example not so often trotted out as Ibsen or
Dumas, is not a thinker, and yet " Die Ehre,"
" Sodom's Ende," " Heimat," while they do not
offer us problems and their solutions, do offer us
presentation of some of the great contrasts and
contradictions of life.

Mr. Pinero's later plays, " Iris " and " Letty,"
will not be called problem plays by any one. " The
Gay Lord Quex " depicts what the marquess himself calls " a curious phase of modern life." So in
an extended sense do " Iris " and " Letty."

" The Gay Lord Quex " can hardly be one of
those plays which we enjoy from its truth to
nature, for few of us have had the privilege of
knowing a social world where a man can flirt with
a manicurist at noon and with a duchess at midnight. Those who can compare the play with life
itself will regard it as a picture of manners. But
more broadly the interest in the play lies in the
cleverness of the intrigue, and in a minor way in
the character of Lord Quex himself. From the
rather doubtful atmosphere of " establishments "
which serve a double purpose, and Italian gardens
and boudoirs which seem to be used for one only,

he emerges with more credit than any one would imagine on his first appearance. But the real thing is the extreme cleverness of the turns in the third act, wherein the manicurist and the reformed rake pit themselves against each other. This is dramatic construction; something which I admire immensely when I see it and consider it impertinent to praise.

" Iris " and " Letty " have as much construction and more real body to them. The phases of life which they present are more general. If we do not know them, we have known others pretty nearly like them. And if not even that, we can see some pretty general principles of life upon which they are based. The first shows us a bit of the world that is dependent on pleasure. Iris and her friends enjoy life while they have money (whereby they can make others minister to their pleasures), but when they lose it, they are all at sea. It is true that Maldonado is a millionaire banker, Kane a working solicitor, and Trenwith goes to work out his destiny in Canada. But there is not much doubt that Maldonado did not work for his money, while Kane, of course, stole his, and as for Trenwith's making a competence in British Columbia in two years, we on this side the water are simply incredulous. Poor old Croker had got to middle a̲ɩ̲ ithout being useful in the world, and so, when he lost the money he had inherited, he couldn't think of anything but being a club secretary, and as for Iris herself, of course that is the whole play, the picture of the weak nature so dependent upon its luxuries that it must follow the easiest path to them.

As for "Letty," it seems to me as strong a piece of work as anything Mr. Pinero has done. It presents no problem but merely an element in life, namely, a glimpse of a world that has run to seed, particularly of an old family which has kept its money but lost its power of behaving decently, or rather, perhaps, has not moved on with the rest of society. With this is contrasted the world in which Letty lives, sordid, coarse, stupid, and yet with the elements of happiness in it. In a way the play challenges comparison with "Sodom's Ende" and "Ghosts." It need hardly be said that Mr. Pinero does not burn in his idea with the atrocious firmness of Ibsen. And it should be said that he is not so convinced of the real excellence of good, honest, innocent life as is the German, and consequently cannot make his picture of it convincing to the audience. Still one follows Letty intently: at first it all seems disagreeable, true, incomprehensible, but it clears up as the play goes on, until finally, in the last half of the fourth act, the aim of the dramatist comes out clearly, and line

after line is added with perfect definiteness and
surety of hand. And the Epilogue, though possibly not absolutely sincere, is really the right thing.

After his great success with "Iris" and
"Letty," Mr. Pinero seemed firmly established as
the representative English dramatist. His plays
were events of the dramatic season in England and
America, and he was becoming known in Germany,
and to a less extent in France and Italy. It was
therefore considered most appropriate when he received the distinction of knighthood. At the same
time William S. Gilbert, Charles Wyndham, and
several other men of position connected with the
theatre received the same honour. Sir Arthur
Pinero was an eminently proper representative of
the drama. Indeed, there has been no one in England to eclipse him.

Some time ago Mr. Jones would have been
thought a rival, but hardly to-day. Mr. Barrie
might be thought of, but his dramatic activity has
not been for long, and his work, though always
called charming and artistic, does not seem to con-
stitute a body of achievement which gives him
an absolute first place. There are younger men,
too, with a play or two apiece, often very striking
things, which one or another will think the greatest
ever written, but even with these, Pinero will on
the whole, like Themistocles, prove the best.

Mr. Pinero's next plays, however (still to use his old style), did not increase his reputation. " A Wife without a Smile " was very coldly received. " His House in Order " was more like himself. The idea of the play was really fine: a woman who has been sneered at and despised by a set of people, the relatives of her husband's first wife, suddenly finds herself in a position that puts them all in her power. She is made to see that there is a finer thing to do than to revenge herself. Pinero himself feels the finer thing and puts it strongly. Perhaps the general appeal of such an idea is not really very wide: at any rate, the play was not such a success as those which followed. In his two latest plays, however, Pinero seems to have regained his old powers. " Mid-Channel " and " The Thunderbolt " may not have excited so much attention as " The Second Mrs. Tanqueray " and " Iris," but the reason for that lies partly in their subjects and partly because they came later.

" The Thunderbolt " is the earlier of the two, and is probably thought the better. I find " Mid-Channel " the more interesting. Both plays are based upon very general elements in life: the first upon people's behaviour in relation to money, the second their behaviour when married and arrived at middle age. These are surely topics which almost every one will appreciate: they are Bernard Shaw's

great topics, property and marriage. Everybody
knows the glow of joy with which they receive
money they did not really expect; many people
know the irritations and tediousnesses that often
come to those who have been married a good while
without having developed any real companionship.
These strike me as better topics than the " problems," as they used to be called, of Pinero's earlier
plays. They are better, too, because more general than the subjects of " Iris " and " Letty."
Pinero, it is true, presents his themes under conditions to which we are not much accustomed, the
middle class of an English provincial town, in one
case, and a rather fast second-rate society in London. But even in these especial forms we can get
a good deal that we feel rings true.

" Mid-Channel " shows the " modern technique "
as it is so often called, the technique of Ibsen that
we read about, the technique that is held to have
driven out the patterns of Scribe. The main elements of the new art are said to be these: the sim-
plifying the way things are brought about, having
no surprising coincidences and so on; the using
no more characters than are really needed to carry
out the action that is planned; and the elaborating
what characters there are to represent elements of
importance in the action. These principles will
strike one at once in the majority of the plays of

the last decade. They are commonly supposed to
have been due to the influence of Ibsen. Whether
they are or not they make a very great difference
in any play in which they are dominant.

Any one who would like to see what these principles result in will do well to compare " Mid-
Channel " with one of Pinero's earlier plays, " The
Benefit of the Doubt." The subjects of the two
plays are not very different: they both concern the
situation of people who, having been married a
number of years, become shaky in their devotion
to each other, think of separating, fall in love with
others, and so on. " Mid-Channel " has, besides
servants, seven characters: a husband and a wife,
a mutual friend, a woman for the husband to go
to and a man to go to the wife, and two others.
It is hard to see how the play could get on with
less, though perhaps one of the two last might be
dispensed with. " The Benefit of the Doubt," however, has many characters: it has a husband, and
a wife who has been called into court as a co-
respondent, and another husband and wife, the
latter of whom has brought the suit. But it also
has all the first wife's family. This family is made
up of characteristic people, a pompous uncle, a
foolish mother, a more foolish son, an independent
sister, a strong-minded aunt, and a convenient
uncle-in-law. And it is chiefly in these other people

that we see the greater concentration of the latter
play. They give life and reality to the situation:
we really do live in a world of a good many people.
They also help present the situation, and in fact
some of them carry on the action. But the other
plan has the greater intensity: given a situation
in which it is natural to have only a few people
about, and the attention directed upon those people
will be more intense. So also as concerns the
mechanism or the management of the action: it
would take too long to analyse the two plays, but
the result here, too, would be that one would see
how Mr. Pinero has made things simpler, and
stronger, by rejecting matters that when we consider them seem a bit unnecessary, roundabout, or
unnatural. In the direction of elaboration of character, I do not know that there is so much to say.
Pinero, to my mind, is never at his best in his
presentation of character. Perhaps he has it on his
mind, but he is often mechanical in it. Thus Zoe
in " Mid-Channel " is presented as a woman who
really loves children, but who agreed with her husband in time past that they had better not be
" bothered with children " in their married life.
But the way this important trait is presented is
simply by two or three references to " the kid-
dies " in Zoe's talk in the first act, and afterward
nothing more about them. Perhaps Pinero merely

meant to present a woman who had vague ideas
that if things had been different she would have
done better, but I hardly think so. So far as I
get his idea, it is that this pair had got apart
from each other because they had denied the plain,
normal impulses that are at the bottom of family
life, and had tried to manage as they fancied, at
first, would be more amusing and interesting and
helpful in making a way in the world.

However one looks at that, though, this play,
one of the latest of Pinero's, is to my mind as good
a thing as he has done. A better subject and better
handled than any of the earlier plays. It shows
a better grasp on life and a better understanding
of dramatic art. It shows a man in touch with
the time and able still to grow. We may put down
something, doubtless, to the dramatic movement
of the last twenty-five years. The play is " modern " and so are we, and so we like it better than
things of an earlier fashion. But with all that much
must be set down to the credit of the dramatist,
who doubtless is to be called not merely the product
of the " modern " movement, but also a part of it.

BERNARD SHAW

It is hard to take Mr. Bernard Shaw seriously, for he has such a gift of wit and paradox that he is apt to seem desirous of appearing frivolous. It is hard also to write about him, for he has written a good deal about himself much more cleverly than most people have written about him. He has a much better knowledge of the subject and a superior gift of expression. Yet the attempt must be made, for he really is serious in the main. He wishes to accomplish something worth while and he will do so, too, or do something in the direction. If one cannot get into touch with him, then so much the worse for oneself.

I was about to begin by saying that Mr. Shaw was not so much a master of stagecraft as some other people. Just then, however, I saw in a paper that a distinguished actor of his plays affirmed him to be greater in dramatic construction than Shakespeare. That made me pause. It is true that the remark was made at the University of Chicago, an institution whence newspaper report is apt to offer us matter much more highly col-

112

GEORGE BERNARD SHAW

oured than the original: still such may have been
the opinion of the actor in question. I do not,
however, believe that it is Mr. Shaw's. Mr. Shaw
himself says somewhere, with his usual candour
and even modesty, that he is not remarkable for
stage technique. His plays, he seems to think,
are technically like other plays. He says that he
is better than Shakespeare in one respect, and here
not a few will probably agree with him, but does
not claim superiority in the matter of stage construction. There is not very much point in the
comparison. Shakespeare made his plays for his
own theatre, which was very different from ours,
and much of his absolute stage technique is to-day
impossible. Take the fifteen scenes (more or less)
in the third act of " Antony and Cleopatra," and
in the fourth; that is something out of the question now, and so it is with some other matters. In
a large way I suppose Shakespeare had more dramatic art than Mr. Shaw; certainly he managed
to write more plays that did and do well on the
stage.

But stagecraft is not Mr. Shaw's particularly
strong point, although, like most literary men who
write plays, he seems to be well settled in the
opinion that he knows quite enough about the
matter for practical purposes. It may be
doubted, however, whether his work is especially

well fitted for the stage. He can write, I suppose, almost anything, and he has written a dozen
plays. Some of them have appeared on the stage,
and that with a greater or less success for the
time. But a determined criticism would probably
show that their success was due not so much to
their dramatic character as to something else.

Mr. Shaw's real matter of importance is not
his dramatic art, but his ideas or his way of thinking. He is a critic and a dramatist, it is true,
but at bottom he is a Radical, a Revolutionist, a
Socialist, I believe. His plays may be successful
as plays, and he is naturally pleased or displeased,
but the real root of the matter is in the ideas. In
fact, I suppose his ideas rather interfere with his
success as a playwright, because they prevent his
taking the stage seriously. He says that he did
not at first, and results would seem to show that
he did not afterwards. He generally cast his
plays " in the ordinary practical comedy form in
use in all the theatres," but we may infer that
he could with equal ease have cast them in any
other form; indeed, his later plays have been of
various kinds.

It seems not unnatural that when a man has
mainly at heart the exploitation of some idea or
conception, and considers the dramatic part of
the business of minor importance, he will not be

a pre-eminent success on the stage. The actor considers the acting and the stage management of immense importance, and the ideas of very little or none at all, and even he does not always succeed.

It would certainly not be worth while to attempt to present a boiling down of Mr. Shaw's ideas. For one thing his object in writing is generally to express them, which he does commonly much better than I should be able to. But, for another thing, he has so many ideas. He is, and for a long time has been, a champion of a different order of society, and as such has not only had many good ideas of his own, but he has expressed them excellently and very amusingly. Add to that all the ideas that he has imputed to Wagner, Ibsen, and others, and you have far too many for a short essay. But still it will be worth making a try at the general nature and character of his ideas as presented in his plays, or at least of his dramatic character.

Mr. Shaw has published seventeen plays. " Widowers' Houses " deals with the position of a man who lives on money used by somebody else in ways he cannot approve. This is a pretty important matter in modern life: it brings in what may really be a problem to many. So many people nowadays—I suppose it was so always—

live on the work of others, that it is rather important to know how the money is employed which gets your bread and butter. " Mrs. Warren's Profession " presents a girl whose mother has educated her with money made in a peculiarly dishonourable manner. This is not so common a case; the particular manner brings up various phases of the question which are so special that the general nature of the problem is largely lost. " The Philanderers," which is called an " unpleasant play," has no definite problem, but is more a satire on what used to be called the " new woman." These ideas we need not discuss: they are but special forms taken by the general motive power of Mr. Shaw's thinking.

It is with Mr. Shaw as with most men: you will best get at them when they are not dead set on some special object. " Arms and the Man " has no special target, and for that reason, perhaps, it was more successful on the stage than Mr. Shaw's earlier pieces. Taking as a setting the vague possibilities for romance offered by Servia and Bulgaria, Mr. Shaw calmly produces a strictly realistic play. He presents the world as it is—not especially in Servia or Bulgaria, for I suppose he has no especial knowledge of those countries—but the world in general, and creates a very amusing satire. It is a satire, and it is

amusing, but it has enough hits at truth to be a
little more than that.   Mr. Shaw gets everybody
off their high horses—the soldier, the gentleman,
the romantic young lady—we see and acknowledge the various pretences and affectations of life
as we have often done before.   Mr. Shaw wishes to
get at the real facts, the real springs of action,
but he does not get much farther than others have
done.   That, I suppose, was the reason that
" Arms and the Man " was not more successful
on the stage than it was.   Its object was satire
but not very vigorous satire, nor on very new
lines.   It was more quaint, I should say, than
anything else.   Still, beside its particular satire,
it has plenty of touches which show the more general purpose of the man.   In the first act, where
the Servian soldier has sought refuge in the room
of the Bulgarian young lady, we see constantly
that we are to have the real thing, tinctured with
epigram, it is true, but still nearer the real thing
than melodrama.

" *Some* soldiers," says Raina scornfully, " are
afraid of death."

" All of them, dear lady," answers the man,
" all of them, believe me.   It is our duty to live
as long as we can, and kill as many of the enemy
as we can."

There is satire and epigram there, but there is

also a certain sort of reality and great reason-
ableness. There is plenty of it. " Bless you,
dear lady," says the man, " you can always tell
an old soldier by the inside of his holsters and
cartridge boxes. The young ones carry pistols,
the old ones grub." It may or may not be so, but
at any rate it is a resolute doing away of conventional romance, of the romance of pictures and
books and so on, for the reasonable view which is
willing to make an effort after the facts. It need
not be that Mr. Shaw knows as much of what real
soldiers actually are as Mr. Kipling. That par-
ticularity is rather beside his purpose: his especial
aim is to open our eyes now and then to the impossibility of carrying through half the notions
that have grown up in the minds of every one from
books and pictures and superficial talk, mingled
with our own childish imagination and self-centred
desire. That sort of thing will not stand the test
of experience; people are always coming to grief
by depending upon it; better open one's eyes and
interpret what one really sees by a little common
sense.

When you have your mind set on this sort of
thing it must be hard to think of doing anything
else. I think it is remarkable that Mr. Shaw
should have any dramatic construction at all. I
remember nothing of it in " Arms and the Man,"

which is, all the same, one of the cleverest and most amusing plays that one reads. I am sorry to say that I never saw it, but I suspect that it does not make quite so much difference as with some other plays.

"You Never Can Tell" is another delightful play. It is on the face of it more frivolous and, indeed, more impossible, if one may say so, than "Arms and the Man," but it is full of the same sort of eye-openers as the other, and in the passages between Valentine and Gloria it begins to get quite close to some of Mr. Shaw's later heresies. That delightful waiter, too,—I'm sure he would have made an Admirable Crichton if he had had half a chance. Let us get on, however, to "Candida," for that is, I take it, the best of Mr. Shaw's plays. It was the most successful both on publication and on the stage. It gave most immediate pleasure and comes most readily to mind. It has both ideas and action.

"Candida" carries the process of eye-opening, so dear to Mr. Shaw, one step farther than "Arms and the Man." First we have the Rev. James Morell, a Christian Socialist, and therefore at war with the many evils and falsenesses of our social life, and intent in bringing in a good, strong, and honest way of life among people who are too much

bent on making money and enjoying themselves
to consider carefully the ways in which they do so.
Certainly the character is inimitably good, and
when we think chiefly of that kind of pleasure that
comes from seeing people and things presented in
a perfectly natural way and with a perfectly sure
touch, aside from what they happen to be, when
we answer with a thrill to every certainty of por-
trayal, and chuckle to ourselves at every small
point of human frailty painted for us just as it
is, why, the Reverend James appeals to us as few
figures upon the modern stage. We have him at
his best in the contrast with Mr. Burgess, the
" man of sixty, made coarse by the compulsory
selfishness of petty commerce "—there we have
him at his best, and he makes the right impression,
a go-ahead, clear-visioned, plain-speaking man,
understanding the world and taking it for what it
is. " Well," he says to his old scalawag of a
father-in-law, " that did not prevent our getting
on very well together. God made you what I call
a scoundrel as he made me what you call a fool.
. . . It was not for me to quarrel with his handi-
work in the one case more than in the other. So
long as you come here honestly as a self-respect-
ing, thorough, convinced scoundrel, justifying
your scoundrelism, and proud of it, you are wel-
come. But I won't have you here snivelling about

being a model employer and a converted man when you're only an apostate with your coat turned for the sake of a County Council contract. No; I like a man to be true to himself, even in wickedness. Come, now; either take your hat and go, or else sit down and give me a good scoundrelly reason for wanting to be friends with me." We certainly have here one who sees through the shams of modern life, and by the very clearness of his vision, somehow, has power to make all others feel all their sham pretentiousness. And as he transfixes the ridiculous commercialist who is trying to make friends with the Mammon of righteousness, we feel that he and we are of those in the front rank of progress, the men who know what is right and so can do it.

And then appears Candida and her poet. He is, to start with, singularly and strangely frank, and strange and singular in other ways. As he and Candida drove from the station he was tormented all the time with wondering what he ought to give the cabman. He is not made to get along well in an everyday world—that is, not as the world considers getting on well.

But it soon appears that the poet is there to show us a range of view above the Reverend James. A poet is a man more sensitive than the rest of the world, and who therefore sees more than most

men, and who has more power of expression and
therefore says what he sees more exactly. James
could of course say good things. " The over-
paying instinct is a generous one; better than the
underpaying, and not so common." " No, no,"
says Eugene, " Cowardice, incompetence," which
it often is, at least in the case of feeing, which
was the thing they were talking about. The poet
opens up on Morell at once, and comes out of each
encounter on top.

" Eugene, my boy," says the cheerful optimist,
who has just learned from Eugene that he loves
his wife, " you are making a fool of yourself—a
very great fool of yourself. There's a piece of
wholesome, plain speaking for you."

To which Eugene answers, " Oh, do you think
I don't know all that? Do you think that the
things that people make fools of themselves for
are any less real and true than the things they
behave sensibly about? They are more true, they
are the only things that are true."

We cannot, perhaps, immediately understand
such a point of view. I will confess that when
" Morell grasps him powerfully by the lapel of
his coat, he cowers down on the sofa and screams
powerfully," I rather sympathised with the bigger
man. And when Morell called him a little snivelling, cowardly whelp, and told him to go before he

frightened himself into a fit, I had enough red blood in me to agree with him. But really, of course, it is not anything especially to admire in a man that he is physically so much more powerful than another that he could knock him into a cocked-up hat. We feel that among our own kind of people (whatever kind it may be) it is nice to be big and hearty and strong, and to feel that we could knock the stuffing out of this or that little fool of our acquaintance. But we never make the comparison broader and think that a good, powerful steam-fitter, or a solid coal-handler, is any better than we because he could do us up. So clearly the Reverend James is not a finer fellow, with all the breadth of chest; indeed, he would be the first to discredit the reign of brute force, in spite of the charms of muscular Christianity.

In fact Marchbanks gives us a second eye-opening, and we perceive that the first was, in a measure, deceptive. Mr. Shaw was playing with us. The first was too easy. It is not so much to see through the deceits and shams of society nowadays. Thackeray and Carlyle are not read by everybody, but their chief standpoints are pretty common property. Indeed it is so much the fashion to look beneath the surface that it is not at all hard to take the pose. But really to know what is what, really to react to the facts of life, to be really genuine, that is no easier than it was in the days of Teufelsdroeckh, or of Gulliver, or of Piers the Ploughman.

Not that the Reverend James is absolutely a pretentious gasbag any more than Marchbanks is an inspired prophet. He has a definite, a positive part in the world's work. You cannot reform the world with a few epigrams; most reformers are impracticable persons, which means that they cannot determine details, do not like to take the trouble to make their ideas fit complicated cases, are puzzled at any specific correct thinking, have not patience and skill absolutely to know anything, except a few general principles, " great laws of life," as their admirers subsequently call them. They are not the people to do the work of reforming the world; the world has to reform itself. But it can only be got to reform itself by middlemen, so that the reformers have to have followers, commonly men who do not entirely understand them, but who get full of better ideas than they had before, at least, and who incite the world to work itself over into something a little better than it was before. The new ideas are handed around in predigested tablets, and get to be rather the thing. Then the original thinkers retire or are retired to the background, and the reign of talkers begins. The Rev. James Morell is a

typical talker. The original thinker is a dreamer
and doesn't like to do anything. The talkers are
commonly men of vitality who have neither the
imagination to dream nor the patience to think for
themselves. They want to do something in this
world, but, having no notion of just what they
can do, they take it out in talking. They believe
absolutely in what they say, while they say it, and
they rouse people to a state of excited conviction
by the hypnotic power of their language, as Mr.
Morell did at the meeting of the Guild of St.
Matthew. It is these latter people, those that
listen to the talkers, who go ahead and do the
world's work in reforming itself; but as they are
creatures of the emotions rather than of the intellect, they never follow people like Marchbanks
because they do not understand them nor like
them, but do follow people like Mr. Morell because
they do like them and do not have to understand
them.

Of course Mr. Shaw is one of the Marchbankses,
but he is not entirely without sympathy for the
Morells. Who can be entirely without sympathy
for them?—big, strong, hearty fellows. How
much better it is that they should earn a living
by talking than that they should have to hoe corn
all day on a farm or dig dirt on a railway. They
do more good, too.

In " Candida " Mr. Shaw sometimes loses the
reformer in the dramatist.   Yet he does not do so
wholly; he certainly shows a sympathy toward the
end for the Reverend James which is not entirely
consistent.   Recollect that scathing description of
his family home.   " You should come with us,
Eugene, and see the pictures of the hero of that
household.   James as a baby! the most wonderful
of all babies.   James holding his first school prize,
won at the ripe age of eight!   James as the captain of his eleven!   James in his first frock coat!
James under all sorts of glorious circumstances! "
That is about as bitter in its satire as we can wish:
Mr. Shaw puts it in the mouth of the man's wife.
That was the right thing to do, and yet he also
allows us to feel a little sympathy for him.

" Candida " is undoubtedly an excellent piece
of writing, full of those flashes of reality that are
the great thing with Mr. Bernard Shaw.   People
sometimes discuss it as a play with all seriousness;
ask about its problem, about the character of Candida, about the poet's secret, and such things.
They are all beside the point.   One may talk of
them if one will, just as one may (indeed must)
admire Miss Proserpine Garland.   But the real
thing in the play is that it gives a standpoint
from which to view the world.

Appreciating this, we may proceed to Mr.

Shaw's latest utterance, " Man and Superman,"
which I saw in the paper the other day is to be
produced in New York shortly with notable omissions. This, perhaps, makes it unnecessary to
write about it at present. The play has been
written, and Mr. Shaw has also written a criticism
upon it, so that no one else need try his hand upon
it. There still remained the possibility of saying
and showing either that it would do on the stage
or that it would not. I was going to say the
latter. But there is no use saying it now if the
play is to be acted before this gets into print.

" Man and Superman " is far more a play of
idea than most of Mr. Shaw's. " Arms and the
Man " gave us an idea of the standpoint of Mr.
Bernard Shaw; he was a realistic satirist. " Candida " went a step farther; it made it clear that
here was a realist and a satirist who was not a
mere promulgator of everyday realism (like Balzac, say) nor of everyday satire (say Thackeray).
Mr. Shaw, it appeared, was an entirely modern
person, an out-and-out advocate of neo-realism.
Neo-realism is merely the presentation of the ultimate facts of life in any way you like. In " Man
and Superman " Mr. Shaw, having pierced to the
secret of the ultimate development of Man from
protoplasm to the Superman, presents it to us in
a piece of extravagance, ostensibly in the garb of

to-day, with automobiles and so on, but really of
an entirely fanciful nature. This mode of presentation is worth remarking: it is almost a note
of Mr. Shaw's dramaturgy. The expedient is
that of a frankly impossible motive carried out in
a very realistic manner. " The Philanderers "
and " You Never Can Tell " were entirely absurd
and impossible in conception, but entirely realistic
in execution. The other plays do not have quite
so much of it, but there is usually some: in " Candida " the calm discussion of which man the lady
is to go with seems almost as though Mr. Shaw
thought it a natural proceeding, but of course it
is not more so than having Cleopatra carried into
Cæsar's presence in a roll of carpet (I hope that
is not historical) or having General Burgoyne
march from Boston to Albany to meet General
Howe. " Man and Superman " is quite as fan-
tastic as any romantic play: the main difference
is that it is not so interesting; the dashing across
Europe in an automobile pursued by the girl one
is destined to marry, and landing among a set of
Spanish brigands, the chief of whom has been a
waiter at the Savoy, serves as a vehicle for Mr.
Shaw's views as well as anything else, but in itself
it has no imaginative character, and, indeed, is
rather a dull sort of humour.

But the form is not a matter of great impor-

tance, though I wish it were really amusing as
Mr. Shaw could have made it. The constant play
of idea is the main thing or else the great idea
at bottom. It is hardly necessary to say that the
true nature of the great truth promulgated in the
play is not easily grasped even in reading, would
be less easily understood if the whole play were
given on the stage, and will not be even guessed
at if the third act is much cut. It is to the effect
that the process of development of man into a
higher form (the Superman) is to be carried on
by sexual selection just as his development from
lower forms has been, and that in this process
women (do or should) wish to get married in order
that they may have children, and not for any
minor motive that fancy or romance or conven-
tionality or policy may try to push into promi-
nence, and that men, having been of use in this
process, have about as much place in the economy
of nature as a sucked orange at breakfast. That
seems a curious idea for a play. Mr. Shaw presents it to us by the spectacle of two young ladies,
one of whom marries secretly and persuades the
father of her husband not to disinherit him, and
the other marries openly, having persuaded her
own father before dying to place her in charge of
the person she had singled out for that purpose.
A slight action is given to the piece by the dash of

the not-yet husband across Europe in an automobile in flight from the girl who intends to marry
him.   All the other characters come after him in
another automobile, and all fall among comic
brigands.

All this circumstance appears to me to be
pretty poor stuff, and I shall take leave of it
merely by saying that, were it a hundred times
poorer, the play would still be worth reading for
the constant cleverness of the dialogue and the
occasional seriousness of the matter conveyed.
The theory of the play I suppose to be entirely
false, but I have no concern with it, one way or
the other.   It gives Mr. Shaw a chance for his
epigram, and his epigram gives us a chance at
getting at a bit of truth now and then, or of
thinking that we do, both of which are exhilarat-
ing sensations.   We need not swallow them all any
more than we swallow the ocean when we go in
swimming,—in fact, we could not do so if we tried,
—but in the constant effort to keep intellectually
afloat and to swim about, we find ourselves ma-
terially invigorated and refreshed.

This realistic brilliancy is the great thing about
Mr. Shaw.   For the moment, I think, everything
else becomes dull and tawny beside this white light.
Pinero seems to be the merest boy, smoking cig-
arettes and talking of things that he knows as

much about as the rabbit does of the purposes of
nature.   Sudermann is evidently one who makes
not even an effort to see beneath the crust of custom and convention of a thousand years.   Hauptmann, with all his brilliancy, is merely the bright
child who amuses you by telling how he gets the
better (or else doesn't) of oppressive elders, a
jam-pot rebel against meat and potatoes.   Rostand is the painter of very exquisite and charming
pictures to illustrate Jack-and-the-Beanstalk and
other such classics.   This man, on the other hand,
has had life under his microscope and knows its
secrets, has put himself in touch with real scien-
tists who know the constitution of the universe,
and who now presents to us, with the sugar coat-
ing that we demand, a few of the ultimate facts of
life, that we may like or dislike, understand or
not, but which are facts.

Such is something like the first impression that
Mr. Bernard Shaw may fairly make on one who
reads or sees his plays.   Not that one will necessarily admire him or care about his ideas, but it
seems very hard to deny them entirely or to get
round them and him.   You are on his side
throughout the play, even if, when it is over, you
are astonished to find what company you have been
keeping.

First impressions and second thoughts are often

different. They are with Mr. Shaw. First impressions will be more or less of the kind that I have described: second thoughts are sure to be anything except that. The particular change that comes over one in regard to Mr. Shaw is that his white light loses brilliancy, and perhaps goes out. That is to say, shortly after you have been decidedly under the influence of his brilliancy, his cleverness, his realities, you find yourself not quite sure just what those ideas were that so short a time ago seemed, if not indubitable, yet at least absolutely there. For this there is a twofold reason.

The first is that, though he writes plays, Mr. Shaw does not present his ideas dramatically. They are as they happen to be stated in the dialogue, they are what they are, that is all,—and enough, too, some may think. But for a dramatist it is not enough. The drama has particular ways of giving impressions. They are very effective ways, and they result often in powerful and long-continued impressions. If, however, a man writes plays and does not avail himself of the possibilities of the drama, then he gets all the drawbacks of the drama without its attendant advantages. And as a means of presenting ideas the drama has one serious drawback, namely, lack of space. The dramatist has the means of com-

pensating for this disadvantage, he can even turn
it to his own purpose. He will make up for his
lack of opportunity in statement somehow; if he
is going to do anything, he will have action, situation, characters to carry the thing, to make it
stay in our mind, to serve us as tokens of the ideas.
If we do not have this, if we merely have the people
on the stage telling each other one thing or another, even if it be in epigrammatic dialogue, we
shall not get any more out of it than we usually
do in hearing people tell of things. We cannot
expect to remember all that we are told; we may
remember or we may not, according as the ideas
strike us at the time. Now " Widowers' Houses "
and " Mrs. Warren's Profession," which are the
two of Mr. Shaw's plays that have the least interesting ideas, are the two of which the idea remains most readily in the mind, because in each
case, what idea there is, is expressed in a dramatic
way. It is embodied in a figure, Vivien returning
to her work at Frazer and Warren's, Trench
shaking hands with Mr. Sartorius; these people
remain in our minds in a manner sufficiently suggestive of the idea that is necessitated by the existence of each. But the other plays do not leave
much of an idea; admirable characters some of
them have, and to be remembered for themselves
(the waiter, the Reverend James, 'Enery Straker),

but not for any ideas implicit in them. So the ideas have to trust to whatever statement of them there may happen to be, and in a drama such statement is always insufficient; sometimes in a good play we have explanations of theory, like Graf Trast's disquisition on honour in " Die Ehre," but generally the dialogue of a play is not well fitted for that purpose. We do not, then, remember Mr. Shaw's ideas very well, and thus in a short time he becomes, as far as any effect is concerned, much like anybody else.

The second reason that his ideas do not affect us much is hardly worth mentioning after the first. It is that his ideas, as a rule, are not such as can in any way be promulgated on the stage. Some ideas can: the constant effort of the idealist, the constant strife of the individual,—these ideas (it is fair to call them so) can be dramatically presented. They may not be worth so much in the practical affairs of life as a correct understanding of the way that man is going to get married in his development into future ages, or the way man should manage whatever marriage he happens to be concerned in now, but they seem to be more susceptible of dramatic presentation. Take a thesis like that of " Man and Superman " or of " Candida," if you can get at it. It will be found to be a social generalisation, which, even to be considered, must be presented either on the basis of reason or of authority. A play is the place for neither. The Germans are apt to think that Shakespeare wrote his plays to present great and often complicated social ideas, but if he did he was wasting his time, for that is not the kind of idea the drama can present effectively. It can present the conception of the disharmony of the man of thought in a world of action as in " Hamlet," the place of young love in an old civilisation that is tired of it, as in " Romeo and Juliet," but those are much simpler notions.

But of course it is of no earthly consequence whether Mr. Shaw is a dramatist or not. He can write most amusing plays, and, now that the whirligig of time has spun a bit, we can see them on the stage. And if we do not always get his Ideas,—or at least do not remember them when we do get them,—yet still something remains. We have had a constant challenge and stimulus, a frequent opening of the window. We shall constantly turn to his work with the desire for reality and the curiosity to know the essential under the superficial, and the assurance that by holding on and constantly purifying our vision, we may see well enough to get a step or two nearer the truth.

Such, it appears several years afterward, was an impression of Mr. Bernard Shaw formed at

the very period at which he was emerging into
" the public eye." For a number of years he had
written all sorts of things, and among other plays,
which had been now and then acted by the adven-
turous, but which were really known only as they
appeared in collected volumes. Now suddenly Mr.
Shaw became a popular dramatist. First, I believe,
in Germany (" Candida," in Dresden, November
19th, 1903 ; " The Devil's Disciple " in Berlin, November 25th, 1904 ; " Arms and the Man " in Berlin, December 8th, 1904) ; then perhaps in America (" Candida," December 9th, 1903 ; " You
Never Can Tell," January 9th, 1905), and finally
in England (" Candida," Court Theatre, April
26th, 1904), did Mr. Shaw's plays become popular
attractions and Mr. Shaw a striking figure in popular interest. This period of publicity continued
for several years, by the end of which time Mr.
Shaw was well established as a " World Figure "
in the domain of literature and art. His novels
were published and republished. Almost everything dramatic of his was either acted or would
have been, had it not been for prohibitions or
popular agitations, which were quite as effective
in getting Mr. Shaw well known as acting would
have been. In a few years this singular popularity
came to an end. The public could not understand
Mr. Shaw and found something more amusing. In

the last year or so Mr. Shaw's plays have not met
with such success upon the stage. But the publicity served an excellent purpose, for it introduced him to many who had not known his work
before and who became immensely interested in
him, so that he is still widely known by the readers
of all countries.

Since the first years of his popularity, Mr. Shaw
has written six plays. Of these " John Bull's
Other Island " was written as a contribution to
the national Irish Drama, and has had, as Mr. Shaw
tells us, " immediate and enormous popularity with
delighted and flattered English audiences." The
next, " How He Lied to Her Husband," is a slight
pendant to " Candida." Next came " Major Barbara," which was given in 1905 at the Court
Theatre, London, although Mr. Shaw tells us nothing of the audiences. The next three seem to have
been written after the spotlight had passed away
from Mr. Shaw and have only received minor presentation: they are " The Doctor's Dilemma," " The
Showing-up of Blanco Posnet," and " Getting
Married." All six are now published, accom-
panied, according to Mr. Shaw's custom, by
prefaces.

These prefaces ought to be especially remarked
in a book on the drama. Mr. Shaw is not the first
to use the preface as a way of exploiting or illus-

trating the ideas of his plays, but he has used the means so much that he has made it practically his own. One of Mr. Shaw's critics points out that the custom has two advantages: the same ideas are as a rule presented in preface and play; the reader who likes plays as such can get the ideas from the prefaces and will be immensely amused at their cleverness, while the reader who does not care to read plays at all will find in the prefaces just as much as the initiated find in the plays. And these are advantages. Still it must be said that if it is more or less indifferent whether one read play or preface, it would seem to show that the main thing in the play was to be found in the preface, namely, that it was not anything especially dramatic. This idea impresses one very particularly in the last volume, in which the prefaces are longer in relation to the play than in earlier works, and relatively more interesting.

Of these later plays of Mr. Shaw I regard " Major Barbara " as much the best. I have not seen it on the stage, and am not very sure of its dramatic character. It certainly lacks something of that " modern technique " one is so constantly seeing mentioned in current criticism. It does have one thing which that technique calls for, namely, characters to carry the theme. These characters are Undershaft and his daughter Barbara. They

are representative of two ideas: Undershaft, " a
man who has become . . . conscious of the irre-
sistible national truth . . . that the greatest and
worst of crimes is poverty " and who has therefore
grown rich by manufacturing cannons and ex-
plosives and other means of destruction; and Barbara, the Major in the Salvation Army, who seems
to be thought of as representative of current
Christianity, which she deserts at the end of the
play for what Mr. Shaw calls " The Gospel of St.
Andrew " Undershaft. Around these people are
others, as farcical and as natural as Mr. Shaw's
people usually are. Undershaft's wife, the daughter of the Earl of Stevenage, a young professor
of Greek engaged to Barbara, another daughter
and the young man she is engaged to, Jenny Hill
of the Army, and two or three people whom the
Army deals with. These different figures are all
means of expressing different ideas, and they all
do express them characteristically and amusingly,
—often in ways that no human being would ever
really adopt, of course, but that is the amount of
farce that Mr. Shaw rather demands for his realism. He is a satirist and few satirists can present
life just as it is and make you see their point.

From the dramatic standpoint, I suppose, the
difficulty is that these people merely talk and do
nothing. That is more and more the criticism that

I read of the plays of Mr. Shaw presented on the stage. I cannot see that there is really any action to " Major Barbara ": Lady Britomart Undershaft wishes to get her husband, who has been long separated from her, to provide incomes for his daughters, which he is quite able and very willing to do; he himself wants to get some successor to his business, and finds in the young man engaged to Barbara somebody who finally desires to take the position. But all that does not make any action that one will be much interested in. The only thing that happens that is of any real interest to Mr. Shaw is that Mr. Undershaft succeeds in convincing Barbara that the Salvation Army is insincere, and her young man that the gunpowder business is fine. The first he does dramatically, as one may say. He gives the Army £5,000, made by selling death and destruction, and Barbara then understands that the Army's begging of money is a point of decay that will make the whole thing rotten. Just how Mr. Undershaft converts the Greek professor is not clear: he shows him his factory and the thing is done. These things are not very convincing, and I presume the play was not very effective on the stage. Its interest lies too entirely in the dialogue and the characters.

Still it is a very interesting play. It is about religion, for one thing, which, as Mr. Undershaft

says, is " the only subject capable people care for."
And if we regard religion merely as a philosophy
of life, we may say that it puts strongly the case
for the religion of selfishness, and also that for the
religion of unselfishness, and does not really decide
between them.   Mr. Shaw in his preface (" First
Aid to Critics," he calls it) says that the play is
about the importance of having money (p. 161).
But no philosopher will choose so unimportant a
subject as that.   Money is nothing in itself: it is
merely as a means of influencing others that it is
interesting.   What Mr. Shaw means by the new
article in Andrew Undershaft's Gospel is that it
is important to be able to command people and
make them do as one likes.   That is what money
essentially is.   You can get people to serve you
by giving them money, for by it they can get others
to serve them.   Undershaft's religion is not the
gospel of property.   It is the Gospel of Power, of
Doing as one Pleases, of Self.   The only thing
remarkable about this gospel, in Mr. Shaw's presentation at least, is that he should think there was
anything new in it.

The other Gospel Mr. Shaw presents less con-
vincingly, of course, because he does not believe in
it, and in fact does not know precisely what it is,
but still with excellent effect.   He presents in the
second act, which is laid in the Salvation Army

Shelter at West Ham, a view of Christianity
which in spite of many absurdities is really more
effective than that which we hear in many churches.
He presents Christianity as a happy, personal relation with the spiritual power that rules the world,
and that is something that many Christians fail
to do. One would suppose that Mr. Shaw did not
believe that there was any such power: if that be
the case, he has certainly entered very sympa-
thetically into the hearts of those whom he has
studied in order to create the characters of Barbara Undershaft and Jennie Hill, for they have in
their few words and actions more of the true spirit
of the Salvation Army than the average reader will
distil out of a hundred *War Crys*. The weaker
side is presented, too, the hypocrisy of the so-called
" converts " on one side, the grasping finance of
the Army itself on the other. But that is fair
enough: those things may be seen in every Salvation Army meeting. If the real thing be there, too,
even in a measure, no one should complain.

So one of these plays, at least, is of the stuff
to which Mr. Shaw accustomed us before he became
popular. The three later plays are not of the
same stuff. " The Doctor's Dilemma " may be supposed to be upon a question that must have occurred to many people: the question as to whether
a doctor ought to use every possible means of

science to cure or keep alive those who offer themselves as patients. There is a " problem " here and
one that could probably be given dramatic treat-
ment. Mr. Shaw has put much that is very amusing and characteristic into his rendering. But the
play suffers from a double aim: if the question
involved is of any importance we ought not to lose
sight of it almost entirely by the middle of the
play; if it is a play about a doctor in love with
a patient's wife, it languishes in the middle and
at the end one does not really know why it turns
out as it does. So one has to fall back upon the
stereotyped remark that the play " is not well con-
structed but certainly forces one to think." " Getting Married " is characteristically clever, the people are some of them excellent, and their ideas
amusingly audacious. The new-woman Lord May-
oress and her hypnotism is quite worthy of Mr.
Shaw. The play, however, had very little dramatic
construction, something which from this time on
Mr. Shaw apparently, and his adherents certainly,
hold in very little regard. " The Showing-up of
Blanco Posnet " has been pronounced " the most
direct and dramatic play " of the three. But to
me it seems so unreal in its imaginary presentation
of our own Wild West, something that Mr. Shaw
evidently knows nothing about, that it quite lacks
" convincingness," as they say so much nowadays.

The book in which the three are published is full
of what is immensely characteristic of Mr. Shaw:
it has splendid prefaces, but the plays are only
plays by courtesy.

A man like Mr. Bernard Shaw calls forth violent
opposition and devoted admiration. He has been
attacked with all sorts of satire and abuse. He has
been compared with Barnum beating his own
drums. He has been called " a vain person who
tottered from the scene with no other companion
than a mirror and a sycophant, stripped, at the
end, of those things which best he loved, flatterers,
photographs, and press-cuttings." He has been
depicted together with Wells, Chesterton, Gals-
worthy, and others as being the inhabitants of
literary London, whom Edmund Gosse exhibits to
the returning shade of Robert Louis Stevenson.
Stevenson says, " And now that you have shown
me your popular preachers and politicians, let me
see some of the men of letters." Mr. Gosse has to
answer, " But, my dear Louis, these *are* the men
of letters."

Mr. Shaw can, of course, defend himself against
such direct and indirect criticism, and indeed does.
Few will doubt, however, that Mr. Shaw is more
or less like Barnum in that he believes in telling
people about himself and his work; that, if not
simply vain, he has a good deal of the egotism

that in one form or another is a necessity with
the man of genius, or that he is much more of a
reformer than an artist. These things, stripped
of satirical figures and illustrations and exaggera-
tions, do not amount to very much. It is true that
we cannot imagine Bernard Shaw working serenely
and perfectly, through decades of neglect, like
George Meredith, any more than one can imagine
his having the delightfully impersonal personality
that Anatole France cannot entirely repress. As
to being an artist, if one mean by that that he
should live in an ivory tower set up in the chaos of
unreason and injustice and unkindness that the
world exhibits, no one would imagine him to be
such a person. That he is just what he is, is not
very strange. People who do not like that sort of
person will behave accordingly, just as water will
sizzle and fizz when the proper things are poured
into it, but that behaviour will not alter the facts
of nature: in fact, it is only one of them.

We may, however, still inquire whether the particular things in question are the most satisfactory
gifts for a seeker after truth. For Mr. Shaw is
nowadays no mere dramatist: he is an Artist-Philos-
opher; he has a mission, a gospel, a message
(though he does not himself call it so); he is an
Interpreter of Life. Let us grant that Mr. Shaw
wishes to bring about reforms in social life, that

a reformer must have confidence in himself in order
to push through the dead mass of popular inertia,
that a man must let people know what he is doing
if he means to accomplish anything with them.
Still is such a person likely to be a good guide
in the pursuit of truth? I rather think not.
Through all Mr. Shaw's work, especially his later
things, I get the feeling of one who writes chiefly
for the joy of contest, using whatever means he
may have at hand at the time.

Still one ought not to be so like a child as to
believe a thing merely because so-and-so says it:
one should be able to do something in estimating
values for oneself. And as has been said, " Better
a glimpse within the tavern caught, rather than in
the temple lost outright." If Mr. Shaw can say
anything that is so, of course it is so, and would
be so even if he announced it in the costume of a
clown at a circus, or painted it on a fence for people to read from railroad trains, or whispered it
esoterically to a few select adulators. The thing
is, What does he say?

Here I must desert the reader, and am glad that
I can confidently refer him to Mr. Shaw himself.
This book has always tried hard to be about the
drama. That is a difficult thing to do with the
literary dramatists of our time, for, like Mr. Shaw,
they are apt to be really more absorbed in their

ideas than they are in their plays. Mr. Shaw says
that " the main thing in determining the artistic
quality of a book is not the opinions it propagates
but the fact that the writer has opinions." This
is true in a sense that is not obvious, but not true
in the sense in which most people will take it. But
whether Mr. Shaw's opinions be important or not,
his main desire is to have people think them over.
He would probably be content with that.

STEPHEN PHILLIPS

"Suddenly, out of a clear sky, the poetic drama is upon us."

Some time ago a gifted and brilliant critic began an article with these extraordinary words. They served him chiefly as introduction to an account of a particular poetic drama which had been produced with "large and wholesome and prudent success" at Pittsburg. But they were inspired by Mr. Beerbohm Tree's acceptance of the play of "Herod," by Mr. Stephen Phillips.

I quote them now, because they made such a singular impression upon me that I think they may appeal to others. They seem to me to represent a very curious critical frame of mind, I think it should be called; a sort of disposition, as it were, a feeling that there is such a thing as "the poetic drama," that its appearance has been earnestly looked and longed for, that by one act of good-natured magic on the part of Mr. Beerbohm Tree, a great consummation is about to come to pass, and that an epoch-making moment is at hand,— or rather was.

148

STEPHEN PHILLIPS

From '' Faust,' a drama, by courtesy of The Macmillan Company.

I may be singular in not having ever held such a
view, but I confess that, though I should be glad
to see more good plays at the theatre, I do not
care a pin to have them poetic dramas.

In fact, when Mr. Phillips seeks to restore
poetry to the English stage, he strives against
wind and tide.   Every great poet of the 19th century tried the same thing and failed.   Coleridge
finally succeeded in getting Sheridan to produce
" Remorse " at Drury Lane; it was successful and
is now not even read.   Shelley chose the drama
mainly as a means for lyric poetry, and should
not be counted.   Keats, Mr. Phillips's forerunner,
—but it would be pressing the matter to say that
he did anything of the sort, though he did write a
play.   So did Wordsworth, though it was never
presented.   Scott's " Doom of Devorgoil " was
by no means as successful as the commonplace
dramatisations that followed upon the Waverley
novels as they appeared.   Browning wrote several
plays for the theatre, and though they were not
failures, they have not kept the stage.   The same
must be said of Tennyson.   As for Swinburne, it
is not probable that he meant his plays for the
stage any more than did Byron, who, however,
appears occasionally in a spectacular " Sarda-
napalus " or a literary " Manfred."

In fact, if we compare the 19th century with

the age of Elizabeth we have a curious contrast.
About 1600 we have a large group of dramatists
who as poets were at least of the second order
(" all but one "), producing plays that appear
to have pleased and delighted the play-going public, while three centuries later we have a series of
poets of greater poetic power than the Eliza-
bethans, who are certainly unable to hold the
stage, or, as a rule, even to obtain a footing there.
Further we may remark that even as literature,
as poetry, the drama of the 19th century is not
comparable to that of the 16th.

Such is the verdict of history which Mr. Phillips or any one else who attempts " the poetic
drama " moves to set aside. If we ask as to the
grounds, we have the rather vague idea that there
ought to be poetry on our stage, that the drama
is the highest form of poetry, that it is a shame
that we cannot have poetry at the theatre as well
as the French or the Germans.

Turning the matter over in our minds, we may
ask why any other poet should think of succeeding in the direction where the most successful
poetry of Shakespeare is a failure. Mr. Bernard
Shaw says that Shakespeare " still holds the stage
so well that it is not impossible to meet old play-
goers who have witnessed public performances of
more than thirty out of his thirty-seven reputed

plays, a dozen of them fairly often, and half a
dozen over and over again." He adds that he
has himself seen more than twenty-three. I do
not doubt the statement, but it is beside the mark.
There is no doubt that perhaps a dozen of Shakespeare's plays hold the stage, but certainly not by
virtue of their poetry. Rather, it may be well believed, in spite of it. Not long ago I saw, as did
many others who were greatly pleased by it, a
very beautiful performance of " Romeo and Juliet " given with wonderful scenery and costume
and very good acting. It is easy to say of such
performances that they are very pretty but not
Shakespeare, but I should not have said so of this
one. It did not give us everything of Shakespeare,
but it did give us much. I do not think that ever
before was I so impressed with the beauty, the
pathos, the tragedy of the old story. But with
all that, the poetry of the play was not there: the
characters, the action, the situations, the settings
were strongly given, but the Shakespearean poetry
seemed absent in spite of the words. In the beautiful scene beginning:

" Wilt thou begone? It is not yet near day,"

we had a strong and realistic presentation, but the
poetry of it seemed to me to have vanished. It may
be that the lines were not very well given, but I

incline to think that the reason for my impression was that the adequate circumstance dulled the imagination, that the realism was too much for the poetry.

Some of the most sympathetic critics of Shakespeare have held some such notion. Lamb could not bear " Lear " on the stage, nor Hazlitt " A Midsummer Night's Dream," and both for the same reason, that the realism destroyed the poetry. So thought one at least who saw " Ulysses " a year or so ago.

> " This isle," says Ulysses,
> " Set in the glassy ocean's azure swoon,
> With sward of parsley and of violet,
> And poplars shivering in a silvery dream,
> And swell of cedar lawn, and sandal wood,
> And these low-crying birds that haunt the
> deep."

Or

> " Little bewildered ghosts on this great night!
> They flock about me—
> Wandering on their way
> To banks of asphodel and spirit flowers.
> Ah, a girl's face! A boy there with bright hair! "

Are not those exquisite passages? Surely, but what have they to do with the theatre? Certainly the stage setting of " Ulysses " was ade-

quate. Many of the scenes were extremely beautiful. I remember the gradual taking form and
shape of the coast of Ithaca as being particularly
so. But for all that the poetry did not harmonise.

To revert to Shakespeare once more. I am
inclined (in my dry-as-dust, academic, mole-like
way) to account for his practical exclusion from
the stage. Managers who watch the public mind
say that Shakespeare generally lacks " heart-in-
terest," that he presents no problems, or something of the sort. But the matter lies deeper.

Shakespeare wrote his plays for a stage very
different from ours. It will perhaps be said that
ours is better, that we can give his plays much
more effectively than the Globe Theatre could do,
and also that Shakespeare would gladly have taken
advantage of our possibilities had he been able.
These things may be so and yet the important
thing is not, say, that we can give Shakespeare
better than his own theatre could, but that we do
give them very differently; and also, not that
Shakespeare would have written with pleasure for
a more developed stage than he had, but that he
did write especially for a stage less developed than
our own.

It is wrong to imagine Shakespeare as an inspired barbarian, his eye in fine frenzy rolling,

pouring out poetry for posterity. What he really thought of posterity in connection with his plays may never be known, but there can be little doubt that he wrote his plays with a definite consideration of just the conditions under which they were to be presented. There was undoubtedly an element of the business man (surely a part of Shakespeare) dealing with the business proposition, namely the Globe Theatre and the Lord Chamberlain's men. It was not that Shakespeare wrote merely to please the public. It was that he knew his powers so well that he could easily please the public and be a poet too. So he dealt with the actual conditions in his own way. Instead of grumbling at the interruptions of his comic actors, he used them for his own ends. Instead of shrugging his shoulders, merely, at the clumsy way in which his boy heroines managed their skirts, he put them into doublet and hose whenever he could. Instead of being cribbed and confined by the simple scaffold of a stage, he used every opportunity given him by the stage-management of his day. Instead of feeling any lack of the scenery with which the masques of Ben Jonson were beautified, he took advantage of the chance for descriptive poetry.

And he produced a drama very appropriate to the Elizabethan stage. That stage relied almost entirely upon the dramatist and the actor. The dramatist provided a mobile and fluent dramatic poem, and the actor presented it with his best ability in declamation and gesture. Our conception of realism at the theatre was unknown. Our idea of spectacle was confined to the amusements of the upper classes.

So far as real conditions are concerned the Shakespearean Hamlet was an actor clad in the costume of his day, standing on a stage in the midst of the audience, even surrounded on the stage itself by a half-circle of spectators. Let us think of that when next we see the melancholy Dane in appropriate costume (of the 11th century or the 16th, as the manager happens to choose) seated on an antique chair on a stage that gives with historical accuracy all the circumstance of the palace of Elsinore. And if we will so think, let us ask whether the poetry written for the situation in which there was nothing else will be likely to satisfy our hearts when our eyes are glutted by the brilliant actuality that has become so important to us.

I think not. The poet at the present day who writes for the stage deliberately puts himself into competition with costume, scenery, and music. Wagner alone has consciously sought harmony in such competition, and with Wagner his music has certainly triumphed at the sacrifice of the rest.

Mr. Phillips may succeed on the stage, but it will be in spite of his poetry and not by reason of it. Let me speak again of the newspaper story, which is typical, if not true. When he read " Herod " to Mr. Beerbohm Tree, the actor-manager listened without remark until he came to a place where there was the sound of distant trumpets. At this he began to have confidence. " He had not known that I had been an actor," remarked with modest pride the poet who had seen pass unnoticed the lines:

" And all behind him is
A sense of something coming on the world,
A crying of dead prophets from their tombs,
A singing of dead poets from their graves.

I ever dread the young."

No, I fear that poetry has no place on our stage and that she will not have, at least just at present. The Elizabethan drama gave poetry to people who could not otherwise get it. It was public poetry, recited for those who could not read. Do we to-day wish to listen to poetry? It may be a doubtful question, but I incline to think that we read so much that we do not wish merely to listen to anything. Who is there when some-

thing is read aloud from a newspaper, but wants to
take the paper and read for himself? Who is
there that having heard a poem from the lips, even
of a good reader, does not wish to take the book
in his own hand and read it. Poetry is hardly
a public art. It is true that Lowell read an Ode
on Commemoration Day and Holmes read many
poems to the class of '29, and we should all be glad
to have heard either. But in the main we like to
have our poetry in the privacy of our firesides,
of our pensive citadels, of our hearts. I have no
desire to hear beautiful poetry in a crowd: I had
rather be by myself and have it alone. So, unless
I am singular in this respect, poetry will not flourish on our stage.

The attentive and logical reader will probably
incline to think that this is a short-sighted view
in a period which has produced the poetical
dramas of Rostand, and various others. I cannot help that. I am not going to try to explain
why the various nations of Europe are different.
The French theatre is different from ours and so
is French poetry. " To what shall we attribute
it," wrote somebody in the *Quarterly Review*,
" that the frivolous and ignorant audience of
Paris, content with a dark and heavy house, a
dirty scene, and six fiddlers, shall listen with
earnest attention to a lifeless translation of

' Philoctetes,' while the phlegmatic and reflecting citizens of London, in a gaudy house glittering with innumerable lights, demand show and song and bustle and procession and supernumerary murders, even in the animated plays of Shakespeare? . . . But, whatever the cause, the fact is undoubted, and whoever writes for the theatre must submit to take it into account." That was nearly a century ago; to-day the circumstances are very different, but not the essential fact. I follow the advice and take account of it in my view that, whatever may be the tendency and nature of the Latin races, the English and Americans do not value poetry at the theatre or anywhere else in public.

Of course it does not follow that because poetry is not for the stage, there can be nothing for the stage but costume and scenery. There is room for much else, and whatever be its name, it is something which will always tend to make the stage finer the more of it there is. There is a passage in Byron's "Manfred" that will illustrate the matter better than I can explain it. It comes in that scene in the Hall of Arimanes where the phantom of Astarte rises and stands in the midst. Manfred speaks:

"Astarte! My beloved! speak to me:
I have so much endured—so much endure—

Look on me! The grave hath not changed thee
    more
Than I am changed for thee. Thou lovedst me
Too much, as I loved thee; we were not made
To torture thus each other, though it were
The deadliest sin to love as we have loved.
Say that thou loath'st me not—that I do bear
This punishment for both—that thou wilt be
One of the blessed—and that I shall die;
For hitherto all hateful things conspire
To bind me in existence—in a life
Which makes me shrink from immortality—
A future like the past. I cannot rest.
I know not what I ask nor what I seek;
I feel but what thou art, and what I am;
And I would hear yet once before I perish
The voice that was my music—speak to me!
For I have called on thee in the still night,
Startled the slumbering birds from the hushed
    boughs,
And woke the mountain wolves, and made the
    caves
Acquainted with thy vainly echoed name,
Which answered me—many things answered
    me—
Spirits and men—but thou wert silent all.
Yet speak to me! I have outwatched the stars,
And gazed o'er heaven in vain search of thee.

> Speak to me! I have wandered o'er the earth,
> And never found thy likeness—speak to me!
> Look on the fiends around—they feel for me;
> I fear them not and feel for thee alone—
> Speak to me! though it be in wrath—but say—
> I reck not what—but let me hear thee once—
> This once—once more!
> *Phantom of Astarte.* Manfred.
> *Manfred.* Say on, say on—I live but in the
> sound—it is thy voice!
> *Phantom.* Manfred! To-morrow ends thine
> earthly ills. Farewell.
> *Manfred.* Yet one word more—am I forgiven?
> *Phantom.* Farewell!
> *Manfred.* Say shall we meet again?
> *Phantom.* Farewell!
> *Manfred.* One word for mercy! Say thou
> lovest me—
> *Phantom.* Manfred!"
>
> (The Phantom disappears.)

I presume that the imaginative, the appreciative, the artistic reader of this passage is always profoundly moved by it. I was never specially moved until I saw the play given upon the stage. Then, amid a good deal of frippery and foolishness, the intonation alone of that last word " Manfred!" gave the whole scene a glory that it has

never lost. In a life in which (like most) much
average work and play, much old commonplace and
new experience tends to dull the keen sense of the
beauty of bygone moments, there remains to me
always the poignant passion of that voice as from
the open tomb, giving an emotion so intense that
current reality, even, fades before it into a forgotten dream. Some readings in Heredia, the sight of
the Winged Victory as she stands at the head of
the staircase, the Garden act of " Tristan," the
first thrilling delight at the pictures of Rembrandt
—not to mention matters that do not belong here
—none have a surer place in my recollection than
this. I could say as Hazlitt said of the Man with
the Glove: " What a look is there. . . that draws
the evil out of human life, that while we look at it
transfers the same sentiment to our own breasts
and makes us feel as if nothing mean or little
could disturb us again."

But this is not the poetry but the situation. And
situation is just what the drama, and especially on
the stage, can give as nothing else can. Everybody
can parallel the case, from the prose drama as
well as the poetic—I could say myself a passage
in the third act of " Sodom's Ende " (" Reinheit!")
as well as the end of the third act of " L'Aiglon."
And those who go much to the theatre count on
such moments, for they are far more a possibility

for the stage than for literature or even poetry.
I cannot recall a case in my seeing Shakespeare
save where Mr. Booth sprang up after the play
in " Hamlet."

But to return to Mr. Phillips. It was probably this electric moment that Mr. Tree noticed
when he heard of the trumpets in Herod. Mr.
Phillips, as a former actor, doubtless knows a dramatic situation. Whether he has power to create
one of the first order is another matter. There
are situations and situations; a single melodrama
may have a dozen. But will they be real ones?
One needs the stage to judge. So far as reading
is concerned, I should say we had one at the very
end of " Herod."

Of course one hopes that Mr. Phillips will
create more, for if he does he is a friend to the
human race, immeasurably lightening its miseries
and adding to its joys. To have a wonderful
possession of that sort is a great thing. Even
so, however, what has it to do with poetry, unless
it be that poetry is smuggled in along with the
drama for literary respectability's sake, as some
earnest critics would have us believe that an idea
may be smuggled into poetry as a sort of ballast?

Mr. Phillips has written very charming poetry,
some lines of which are apropos here. They
occur in the words of Idas to Marpessa.

" Not for this only do I love thee, but
Because infinity upon thee broods;
And thou art full of whispers and of shadows.
Thou meanest what the sea has striven to say
So long, and yearnéd up the cliffs to tell;
Thou art what all the winds have uttered not,
What the still night suggesteth to the heart.
Thy voice is like to music heard ere birth,
Some spirit lute touched on a spirit sea;
Thy face remembered is from other worlds,
It has been died for, though I know not when,
It has been sung of, though I know not where.
It has the strangeness of the luring West,
And of sad sea-horizons; beside thee
I am aware of other times and lands,
Of birth far back, of lives in many stars.
O beauty lone, and like a candle clear
In this dark country of the world! Thou art
My woe, my early light, my music dying."

Those are very beautiful lines, but if they rightly
represent Mr. Phillips' power, do they not mark
his language at least as not dramatic?

But if a man write dramas—poetic or not—
for which the stage can do but little, it does not
follow that the dramas are without value. Of
course the judgment of half a dozen theatrical
critics or of a whole theatrical audience will never

establish that. They may say, or show clearly by their actions, that the play is not suited to the stage,—of which the purpose is not so much, as an eminent lover of the theatre is said to have remarked, " to hold the mirror up to nature " as it is rather to offer the public a very special and delightful kind of pleasure. But a drama may not be in the least suited to the stage, and yet be a very good thing for all that. There are and have been many stages—Greek, Elizabethan, French, our own, not to mention Chinese and Japanese; no play was ever written that could suit them all, although each form of theatre must offer some opportunity for creating the true dramatic thrill. A play cannot be good for all; perhaps it may be good for none, and yet be a source of very great pleasure to " those that like that sort of thing."

Just what that sort of thing is, is not a very difficult matter to state. There is a convenience in the dramatic form that enables some men to express themselves better in that way than in any other. Browning was a man of that kind: he had a curiosity in regard to life and a sympathy for living people that made him enter into his characters and speak for them, as it were. He did so in his first poem, " Pauline," which was a monologue; in his second, " Paracelsus," which was a dramatic poem with no possibilities for the stage; and he did so in "Strafford," which he made a regular stage-play for Macready. Then—if I may touch dangerous ground for a moment—he wrote "Sordello." Tennyson, the story goes, said he understood but two lines in this poem—the first and last—and that neither was true. Now, the lines are as follows:

"Who will may hear Sordello's story told."

"Who would has heard Sordello's story told."

It may be admitted that "Sordello" is not a very simple narrative, but it certainly is a narrative. The lines are quite true, for the story is told—well or ill, of course—that is, it is not in dramatic form. Browning explains this at the beginning of the poem, in a passage which was presumably beyond Tennyson's comprehension, but which now, thanks to sixty years of Browning clubs, will be as clear as cosmic jelly.

> "Never, I should warn you first,
> Of my own choice had this, if not the worst,
> Yet not the best expedient, served to tell
> A story I could body forth so well
> By making speak, myself kept out of view,
> The very man as he was wont to do,
> And leaving you to say the rest for him."

That puts the matter fairly enough: Browning liked to let the man speak for himself, so he commonly wrote in dramatic form. When he undertook to tell the tale himself the results were not so good. The same desire came over Tennyson as he grew older, and, though his earlier poems are mostly narratives, his later volumes are full of dramatic poetry. Every dramatic poem is not a play, but a play is dramatic poetry of the most developed and fullest kind. Browning and Tennyson both wrote plays as well as other forms of dramatic poetry, and so have various poets, often without much thought of the stage, like Byron.

After all, why not? I think some of Mr. Phillips' best poetry is in his plays. I have quoted lines from " Ulysses " and some from " Herod." Here are some from " Paolo and Francesca ":

Francesca. " All ghostly grew the sun, unreal
    the air,
Then when we kissed.
Paolo. And in that kiss our souls
Together flashed, and now they are one flame,
Which nothing can put out, nothing divide.
Francesca. Kiss me again! I smile at what
    may chance.
Paolo. Again and yet again! and here and here.

Let me with kisses burn this body away,
That our two souls may dart together free.
I fret at intervention of the flesh,
And would clasp you—you that but inhabit
This lovely house.
 Francesca. Break open then the door,
And let my spirit out."

I have not seen the play acted. But those who
saw it on the stage, did they not perhaps " fret at
interference of the flesh "? It would seem as if
it might well be so, as one reads that fourth act.
After all, is it the actual love affair that attracts
us, that common intrigue so like a thousand others
save for the intensity of its passion? Do we want
to see two live, beautiful, charmingly dressed
young people in each other's arms? I think
hardly. It is the essence of the poetry, the soul
going out of itself, that we want, and that is in
the lines. There is another " Francesca " on the
stage, and that, I am told, has too much real blood
in it. I should think it likely. Real blood, like a
real pump or any realistic setting, distracts the
mind, which for the time would be conscious only
of its own emotion. It is like a magic-lantern
show going on with the curtain raised and daylight coming in.

In spite of criticism like the above, Mr. Phillips'
plays have still been produced upon the stage.
" Nero " was most elaborately presented by Beerbohm Tree, and afterward " Faust." In the latter
play Mr. Phillips collaborated with Mr. Comyns
Carr. At about the same time as this last Mr.
Phillips produced an adaptation (as it was called)
of Scott's " Bride of Lammermoor," but the criticisms that I have seen of these two latter pieces
were rather unfavourable, so far as their poetical
character was concerned.

On the other hand " Nero " was a most interesting piece. Possibly the kind of interest it excited
would be thought not wholly dramatic, or, indeed,
not even poetic. It certainly had poetry in it,
the most beautiful being chiefly in the speeches of
Agrippina, where Mr. Phillips, with the most perfect feeling, put into the mouth of the mother
parting from the son who has already decreed
her death, some of his most beautiful lines. It has
its dramatic situations, too, though as the play has
not been given in America, those remain, with me,
conjectural. But one of its chief interests is, as
one may say, historical: it lies in the embodiment
in the person of Nero of a type of decadent well
known in the last few years of the nineteenth century. There is hardly a trait in the famous maniac
in Mr. Phillips' play that cannot be paralleled from

the literature of the " æsthetic " movement. From
the fatuousness of his first utterances:

" This languor is the penalty the gods
   Exact from those whom they have gifted high "

to the folly of his last,

" I have given thee flaming Rome for the bed of
         thy death
      O Agrippina "

we have the whole gamut of æstheticism, *toute la
lyre,* as more famous ones have said. It is all
there, gay absurdity, intense emotion, earnest un-
realism, simple childishness, erudite dilletantism.
It is a wonderful figure: perhaps a satire, perhaps
a creation.

   Still, in spite of such things, it seems as if Mr.
Phillips did not wholly appreciate the nature of
his great gift. Take " The Sin of David," for
instance. The story is that familiar to us from
the Bible. By the way one may note that Mr.
Phillips might well have chosen to present it in
its original form: in the very persons of David,
Bathsheba, and Uriah. One who could deal so
imaginatively with Herod and his epoch could
surely have presented something worth while of

the earlier flowering period of the Israelitish mon-
archy and hero-time.   As it was, Mr. Phillips
chose to lay his scene in the time of the Common-
wealth and for David we have Sir Hubert Lisle,
commander of the Parliamentary army in the Fen-
lands in the year 1643.   He falls in love with
Miriam, wife of Colonel Mardyke, whom in the
opportunities of military service he sends to his
death.   He marries the widow, and as with David,
the child born of this lawless union dies in early
years.

There is much that is poetic in the play.   But
there is one thing also that is not often poetic
(and so there is in " Pietro of Siena "), and that
is conciseness and condensation.   Modern poetry
is not often concise or condensed, and poetry of
the imaginative kind of Mr. Phillips seems rather
to demand room for expansion.   One feels in reading these later plays as though one would like
(with Keats, who understood this kind of poetry
well) more room to look about in, more space to
enjoy oneself with flowers and fancies, more than
just what is needed to carry the story.

Yet this conciseness Mr. Phillips apparently
uses of set purpose.   He aims to be dramatically
suggestive.   For instance, take the scene between
Sir Hubert, the Parliamentary David, and Miriam,
the soldier's wife, when they first meet.   It is a

scene of some thirty or forty speeches, none long,
some but of two or three words. Each is admirable and the whole scene is full of a sudden mingle-
ment of foreboding, fear, and awakening passion.
Nature is responsive in its heavy hush, as though
before the storm. And at just this moment comes
the musketry of the shooting of Lieutenant Joyce,
condemned to death by Sir Hubert for violence
to a maid. All is significant, almost every word.
But, one might say, it is almost too significant:
there is not enough poetry to carry the significance
of the situation. It is too purely dramatic: we
need the people, their gesture, their attitude. Singularly strong, one says, though perhaps even on
the stage there is not enough material to carry the
essential, it seems as if it would pass too quickly.

All is simple. That certainly is in keeping with
dramatic usage at present. There is no action but
the main action, and whatever minor act may suggest or illustrate. There are some characters who
have little connection with the main action, but
they are really more background and setting than
characters, officers, and soldiers of the Parliamentary army. All that is like Ibsen, for instance,
or indeed like almost any modern dramatist compared with the dramatists of fifty years since, when
sub-plots, perhaps merely for humorous or lighter
purposes, were common, and also wholly unneces-

sary characters who had nothing to do with the
play, except to be humorous or eccentric, is something of the sort.   Dickens shows that sort of thing
to a very great degree: his plots are the very re-
verse of simplicity, and his characters, though they
usually have something to do, are always most interesting on their own account.   And though Dickens was not a dramatist, and had no reason for
being led by dramatic tradition, yet he shows
in this respect a general artistic tendency of
the time.   And in his classic simplicity and conciseness Mr. Phillips shows a dramatic tendency of
his.

To judge dramatic quality is one of the most
difficult of things, to be able to say what will be
effective on the stage.   If one only could tell on
reading what was going to " do " on the stage,
what a great thing it would be for theatrical managers.   I think that dramatic quality, that which
on the stage makes the lasting impression, must
be not words—whether poetry, epigram, or wit—
but situations, actions, characters, real people in
real relatior of life doing real things.   Perhaps
Mr. Philli‚ ᵢn these later plays lacks in power
of conceivi᛫ character; his figures are certainly
not very original, indeed seem rather typical than
otherwise.   But his situation and his action would
seem to be dramatic, though perhaps lacking in

some quality that would make them more successful on the present stage.

This matter of dramatic quality is one where
there is doubt and difficulty. But poetry is something that one can recognise in books, because it
is there we are accustomed to find it. And we can
say of Mr. Phillips' later plays—" Pietro of
Siena " as well as " The Sin of David "—that
there is less poetry in them, in quantity. And
that is a pity, for Mr. Phillips' poetry, whether
in dramas or not, is very beautiful. He is one of
the few men who have the gift of writing such
words as will arouse the imagination into that tense
consciousness in which we seem to move in worlds
not commonly realised, and to become dimly aware
of things that are ordinarily beyond the reaches
of our souls. Life and the emotions of life seem
richer and finer. It is not that we comprehend
some new idea, or that one thing or another seems
more significant. It is rather that the things we
are accustomed to are seen in a more imaginative
way. And that is what lovers of poetry like.
They want to have moments different from other
moments. And that is something that Mr. Phillips
has often given us, and can still give us. I trust
I may be allowed to express a personal hope that
he will soon do so in ways other than the drama.

MAETERLINCK

It was some years before M. Rostand became
a familiar figure in the literature of the time that
M. Maeterlinck appeared, and in a very different
manner. Although a dramatist, he became known
from the printed versions of his plays. It was in
1893 that translations of his earlier plays were
published in America, and up to that time few in
this country had ever heard of him, fewer were
acquainted with his work, and none had ever seen
his works upon the stage.

M. Maeterlinck was introduced to the wider
world of letters under the cloud of comparison
with Shakespeare. In America and England, at
least, he was therefore received with a smile, as one
of those humorous " movements " that flutter after
each other like exquisite humming-birds through
the Parisian world of letters. He had been called,
by M. Octave Mirbeau in the *Figaro*, the Belgian
Shakespeare. If he had been called the Ollendorf
Shakespeare, the Puppetshow Shakespeare, or the
Nursery Shakespeare, the name would have conveyed more accurately the impression which he

MAURICE MAETERLINCK

made at first. Some people became very angry at
him: Max Nordau, a violent person of that day,
called him a mental cripple, an idiotic driveller,
an imbecile plagiarist. In general, people merely
could not understand him at all, though they could
see that some of his ways were funny. The well-
known dialogue—people may not remember that
it was quite as remarkable as the burlesques on it:

MALEINE

" Wait! I am beginning to see.

NURSE

Do you see the city?

MALEINE

No.

NURSE

And the castle?

MALEINE

No.

NURSE

It must be on the other side.

MALEINE

And yet . . . There is the sea.

NURSE

There is the sea?

MALEINE

Yes, yes; the sea. It is green.

NURSE

But then you ought to see the city. Let us look.

MALEINE

I see the lighthouse.

NURSE

You see the lighthouse?

MALEINE

Yes; I think it is the lighthouse.

NURSE

But, then, you ought to see the city.

MALEINE

I do not see the city.

NURSE

You do not see the city?

MALEINE

I do not see the city.

NURSE

Do you see the belfry?

MALEINE

No.

NURSE

This is extraordinary."

It was, very. There were undoubtedly things to be said for such dialogue; still it was funny, though not uproariously so. Then his princesses,

the babies with long hair: in one piece seven of
them, each as infantile as all the others put together—no one takes them seriously. There was
certainly a good deal that was humorous about
M. Maeterlinck.

Nor did those who admired his work always hit
upon just the right things. I will here mention
myself, merely as an example of one who was much
taken with M. Maeterlinck's first writings and yet
was quite unable to see what has turned out to be
the important thing in them. It chanced that
another poet published about the same time a col-
lection of dramatic pieces which resembled in some
ways M. Maeterlinck's plays. It is not important
whether or no they were imitations—probably not.
But they were very like them, and I allow myself
to quote a few lines written some years ago about
them.

It was under the title "The Antennæ of
Poetry," and although the article itself showed
little critical keenness or foresight, the title, as
appeared later, was not a bad one. In my then
view people like Maeterlinck were experimental-
ists, and fulfilled a useful function in poetry, or
any other kind of art, being always on the lookout
for things that were new, amusing, or edifying.
And in what they offered, as in these cases, the
interesting thing lay largely in the mode of ap-

preciation or presentation. " They are not conceived," I remarked, " in any approach to the
classic manner, but in a manner ultra-romantic.
For although the main emotion is always present
before us, it is not presented simply, but always
by means of a multitude of extremely fine and delicate nuances, indefinite hopes and fears, presentiments, imaginings and spiritual accompaniments,
premonitions almost occult, faint ripples of emotion, little wavelets that skim over the waves of
passion." Such to my mind was the characteristic of Mr. Sharpe's work, and of M. Maeterlinck's, too, except that the latter was more of a
true dramatist, having greater power of drawing
character.

It was not very clever of me to have found
nothing more to say on the first five plays of M.
Maeterlinck. That I should have entirely missed
the real purport of his idea and been wholly taken
up by the accessories, shows one of the practical
difficulties that any one has to meet in dealing with
a new effort of romanticism. What I noticed, the
general tone and method, the character-drawing,
all that amounted to nothing; M. Maeterlinck
would have been himself without either quality.

One thing in the article, however, was, I believe,
good, and that, as I have just said, was the title.
Not in precisely the manner in which I conceived

it, but still in a way near enough to mention was
the name significant. And this I say, not because
I think so myself, but because almost the same
phrase was afterward used by Maeterlinck in
" Le Trésor des Humbles," published some time
afterward, when he spoke of Novalis as " one of
those extraordinary beings who are the antennæ
of the human soul." That was not precisely the
same thing, but it came rather near it. I was
thinking of poetry, and Maeterlinck was thinking
of life. As it turned out, that was the main line
of his interest. People who considered him only
as a curious experimenter in dramatic form were
wrong about him, as also those who bothered their
heads and their readers by talking about symbolism. Symbolist he may have been to some degree,
and experimenter, and various other things. But
in the main his interest was in philosophy, and has
been ever since. He writes plays or studies the
habits of bees, not merely as diversions, but as
means of expression or attainment of something
concerning the problem of life.

Before the publication of " Le Trésor des
Humbles," M. Maeterlinck had been known as a
philosophic man of letters. Every serious author
is more or less philosophic; he has something to
say of the general principles of life; he can hardly
avoid having some philosophy, although he may

make no effort to state it systematically or even
directly. In this new book, however, M. Maeterlinck became a literary philosopher and sketched
for his readers his theory of life. The remarkable thing about the book was not that M. Maeterlinck should have a philosophy, but that he should
try to express it definitely, for the main idea on
style of his previous work had been that his
thoughts were not such as could be definitely expressed, and indeed that idea was rather the
foundation of this book. Still, for all that, by
" Le Trésor des Humbles " M. Maeterlinck presented himself as a philosopher of a known school,
and his work was seen to have a place in a known
tendency of our time.

M. Maeterlinck now appeared to be a mystic.
The name Mystic is a vague one and comprehends
people as far apart as Plotinus and George Fox.
Mystics are perhaps not much farther known than
as they are known to be mystics. Still the word
gives us some idea of a standpoint. A mystic I
take to be a person who believes in the acquirement
of truth by intuition rather than by any process
of reason and argument. Thus the person who
sees visions is a mystic, the person who has presentiments, the person who has something borne in
upon him. Any one who believes in gaining truth
by some process more direct than the ordinary

process of rational thought is, in so far, a mystic.
There have been Christian mystics and mystics
who were not Christians; the word has been very
loosely used. M. Maeterlinck, like others in what
was called in those days the neo-Christian movement, had been interested in Carlyle and Emerson,
but also by those more commonly thought of as
mystics—Eckhard, Ruysbroek, Boehme.

His particular view, however, as presented in
" Le Trésor des Humbles," was not the mysticism
of any of these. It was, I believe, his own. " It
is idle," says his book at the beginning, " to think
that by means of words, any real communication
can ever pass from one man to another." How,
then? By Silence: in the great silent moments
of life, such moments as everybody knows, experienced in love, sport, work, religion, not necessarily
moments of great emotion, but moments in which
we seem to become aware of much. It is M.
Maeterlinck's idea that in such moments we may
become aware of much; indeed, that in such moments only do we get to know anything worth
knowing. Those who attune themselves to such
moments, who learn to use them, find deep mean-
ings in presentiments, in the strange impression
produced by a chance meeting or a look (the
words are in the main Maeterlinck's own), in the
secret laws of sympathy and antipathy, of elective

and instinctive affinities, in the overwhelming influence of the thing that had not been spoken.

The precise view of the universe which M. Maeterlinck held to result from such moments, or from such receptivity, need not be stated just here. What is of interest now is to show the dramatic side of it. It is obvious that such an idea has dramatic possibilities. In the matter of conveying an idea without saying anything—by the secret means of sympathy, instinctive affinity, strange impression—Mme. Sarah Bernhardt would seem to be a mystic of the first water. It was not precisely such powers, however, that M. Maeterlinck had in mind when he thought of the drama as a means for the expression of his idea. What he had in mind he said in an essay on " The Tragical in Daily Life," a short statement which put a whole dramatic art into a nutshell. For a philosopher of M. Maeterlinck's type the essay is singularly definite and logical in its arrangement.

First, as to subject: must it always be some violence? " Does the soul flower only on nights of storm? Hitherto, doubtless, this idea has prevailed." But a new idea is becoming known, and he turns to painting to show that Marius triumphing over the Cimbrians, or the assassination of the Duke of Guise, is no longer the type. The painter " will place on his canvas a house lost in the heart

of the country, an open door at the end of a
passage, a face and hands at rest, and by these
simple images will he add to our consciousness of
life, which is a possession that it is no more possible to lose." Nor will the drama deal with extraordinary convulsions of life; why should the
dramatist imagine that we shall delight in witness-
ing the very same acts that brought joy to the
hearts of the barbarians, with whom murder, out-
rage, and treachery were matters of daily occurrence?

So much for subject: next, M. Maeterlinck
spoke of action, or, rather, the lack of it—and
presented his view of a " static theatre," namely,
a drama in which there was no action at all, a
view which followed naturally from his conception
of subject, which suggests the question, Are these
motives suitable to the drama? It has only been
shown that they are possible in painting, which
is something very different. It is under this head
that one comes on the *locus classicus* of the static
dramaturgy.

" I admire Othello, but he does not appear to me
to live the august daily life of Hamlet, who has
time to live, inasmuch as he does not act. Othello
is admirably jealous. But is it not perhaps an
ancient error to imagine that it is at the moments
when this passion, or others of equal violence, pos-

sesses us, that we live our truest lives? I have
grown to believe that an old man, seated in his
armchair, waiting patiently, with his lamp beside
him; giving unconscious ear to all the eternal laws
that reign about his house, interpreting, without
comprehending, the silence of doors and windows
and the quivering voice of the light, submitting
with bent head to the presence of his soul and his
destiny—an old man who conceives not that all
the powers of this world, like so many heedful
servants, are mingling and keeping vigil in his
room, who suspects not that the very sun itself is
supporting in space the little table against which
he leans, or that every star in heaven and every
fibre of the soul are directly concerned in the movement of an eyelid that closes, or a thought that
springs to birth—I have grown to believe that he,
motionless as he is, does yet live in reality a deeper,
more human, and more universal life than the
lover who strangles his mistress, the captain who
conquers in battle, or ' the husband who avenges
his honour.' "

And finally as to the dialogue. It is the common opinion that the words of a play should be
directed especially to the action of the play, and,
theoretically, one would be likely to say that there
should not be any word at all that should not get
the action ahead. M. Maeterlinck pronounces to

the contrary. The only words that count in his
view are those that at first seem quite useless. It
is the words which are caused by the demands and
necessities of the case that are as insignificant as
the action itself. Who thinks that the best conversation at dinner consists in asking for the
salt, or saying you will have some bread? Here
the only words of high worth are the useless ones.
So in the drama, says M. Maeterlinck, who, by
the way, does not use so material a figure. It is
the super-essential meaning that we must open
our ears for; it is that which we must get if we
are to get anything at all.

All of which is very systematically reasoned out
on a basis not at all difficult to understand.

What, then, were the dramas made upon this
basis, so different from the common theory of the
day? A theme from the simplest daily life, an
action where nothing happens, a dialogue where
the only words of value are the meaningless ones.
One will readily suppose that any drama made on
such principles will excite all the astonishment
that was shown on the first appearance of the
plays of Maeterlinck.

It will be a surprise to those who do not remember, to learn that the only plays of M. Maeterlinck's first publication that were received with
scoffing were those in which he did not carry out his

principles, so that people could recognise them.
" La Princesse Maleine " and " Les Sept Princesses " were the two of his first four dramas that
excited great derision.   But " Les Aveugles " and
"L'Intrus "—where theme, action, and dialogue
follow his own ideas—were received with respect.

The first-mentioned plays do not, ostensibly at
least, carry out M. Maeterlinck's ideas.   What is
the action of " La Princesse Maleine "?   Marius
and the Duke of Guise shrink into insignificance
in comparison with this little lady who goes
through battles and murders to sudden death.
How is it with the " Seven Princesses "?   If their
souls do not flourish in a night of storm it is certainly in a period of strange agitations.   In these
two plays we have nothing simple, natural, normal; all is as wild as the delights of our despised
ancestors.

But in " L'Intrus " it is not so.   It is not a
remarkable scene, only a family around the evening table.   Nothing remarkable occurs; indeed,
nothing at all occurs, that we can see.   Nothing
is said of any importance save as we happen to
perceive the importance of chance words, and yet
what a powerful little piece it is.   How it goes
on the stage I do not know (nor much care till I
may chance to see it), but one cannot read it without feeling its power.   " Les Aveugles " is not

quite so consistent; it is not a matter of ordinary occurrence for a priest to lead a party of the blind whom he is overseeing, into a wood, and then suddenly die. But the piece is almost as effective as the other.

These two pieces made their impression with perfect sureness, even though conceived according to the curious theories we have just noted. It is true that the ideas which they conveyed were not hard to grasp: the approach of death, the position of humanity with a dead church. There may have been ideas signified in " La Princesse Maleine " and " Les Sept Princesses," but they could not be so readily imagined. Yet M. Maeterlinck's theory was, in a measure, justified by these two failures, for whatever ideas these plays may have meant to convey was lost in the extravagance of the subject and the action, even though the dialogue was as simple as in the others.

Indeed it is now apparent that, in spite of theory and in spite of failure, these two were the typical pieces. The others presented, curiously, it is true, but by a symbolism by no means uncommon, ideas that could readily be expressed in other ways, and have often been so expressed. " There is a stillness of death," says the Father in " L'Intrus," and reminds us that it is all based upon a common and everyday conception, and that it represents no new truth and indeed no truth at all. The ideas are common and have been often expressed. It was M. Maeterlinck's desire to present ideas that had not been expressed, that could not be expressed by common means. Let us imagine that he wished to convey something in " La Princesse Maleine " and in " Les Sept Princesses "; it is not necessary, nor at present useful, to try to determine what it was, but the very nature of the plays leads us to the belief that it was not anything that could be conveyed by usual dramatic methods.

With this idea in mind we may turn to " Pélléas et Mélisande." We shall find it in form at least, like the plays just mentioned, something contrary to the theories of dramatic art which the author had put forward not long before. But as those theories were founded upon a definite and intelligible system (however we may disagree with it), we may be sure that the opposition is but superficial. " Pélléas et Mélisande " is a play of love and revenge, like various others; it has a sufficiently definite action, like an ordinary play; it has a dialogue which carries that action along, as the common stage dialogue does. It would seem that M. Maeterlinck had persuaded himself that what appeared to be characteristic in " L'Intrus " and " Les Aveugles " was not essential, that he could gain his effects in the manner of a conventional play. He therefore has ordinary subject, action, dialogue. If we would get at his idea, then, we must neglect these conventionalities and see what is left.

The story of a man whose wife falls in love with his brother is not essential; if it were we should suppose that M. Maeterlinck had something essential in common with Stephen Phillips, which would probably lead us into neglect of the chief virtues of each. The strange region of romance with its castles and caverns, its midnight meetings and violent murderings, that too is not essential; if it were, we might imagine that we had to do with a man like M. Rostand or Hauptmann, though this is pre-Raphaelite romance and theirs is romance of very different kind. But the story, the setting of " Pélléas et Mélisande " have too much in common with other plays for us to think that they are of prime importance with M. Maeterlinck. They are the very things he pronounces to be useless. If we neglect these matters, what is left?

Into a dark, and old, and melancholy world, a world not utterly without gleams of sunshine and a flower or two, but still constrained to its gloom by its own people, and by the people of ages long past, into such a world comes a spirit of beauty from a faraway and unknown place. Here

in this gloomy world are such people as we know:
a powerful, active man, a child, an old man whose
wisdom has taught him only that the riddle of the
universe is unsolvable, and a young man. Whatever the relations of these people may have been,
they are disturbed by the newcomer; the new charm
and beauty bring delight but also discord. It is
the young man that especially understands this
new companion; the feeling of others is but external and superficial, his understanding is vital.
But conditions are such that they cannot be to
each other what they might, and both perish; leaving the world much as it was before, save that there
is a remembrance left of the exquisite and beautiful one, who will some day take the place now made
vacant.

It is not very difficult to see what there is in that,
—all that need be said is that M. Maeterlinck does
not deem it necessary to make it very obvious. He
is content to give us his drama—there must be
some action, characters, dialogue—and to suggest
to us continually matters of wisdom and destiny
that cannot be put in straightforward words without losing some of their truth; to present to us
the possibility of a life of the spirit which shall be
fuller and more beautiful than the life to which
we are accustomed. Is it then beautiful to love
your brother's wife? we may ask. M. Maeterlinck

presumably believes that to love any one is beautiful. He presents spiritual things by common means; he wants to convey the idea of a love which overrides the barriers of the intercourse to which we are accustomed. The barrier of marriage seems to be the one which commonly occurs to him, but in itself that is but an accident, resulting perhaps from lack of imagination, perhaps from other causes. He wants to present to us an intercourse of the spirit and by the very nature of the case he must depict it in some physical form; in just what form is not important.

But let us not rush upon the notion that we must seize the mystical meaning, bear it forth and feast upon it alone. The symbolism has its story which is necessary to it. Why does the soul have a body? We may not be sure, but we know that since it has, we must admit it to consideration. M. Maeterlinck's play is a play even without regard to any symbolism at all. " As it was presented yesterday," wrote somebody when Mrs. Patrick Campbell gave it in London, " at the Royalty Theatre, you felt the poetry of idea, the delicacy of suggestion, the rarity and remoteness of it all. What does it all mean? Anything beyond what lies upon the surface? Perhaps, but at a first hearing, at any rate, you are content to enjoy the beauty, the romance of Maeterlinck's creation."

We may enjoy the externals thoroughly, even though the essential continually haunts us with a vague sense of heightened significance.

M. Maeterlinck's following plays may be readily appreciated after " Pélléas et Mélisande "; we have the same externality and the same suggestion of spiritual life and conversation. In " Alladine et Palamides " we have the same contrast between gloomy castle and bright world, the same conflict of lovers with the rigidity of common life. The story is not precisely the same as in " Pélléas et Mélisande," but there is quite as much love, jealousy, and death. These we need not wish away, as Keats says, but we should take them for what they are worth, and fix our desire upon the spiritual content, the super-expressive element to which we shall respond only by calming ourselves of outward thrills and emotions. " Aglavaine et Sélysette " is not very different at bottom, though the mise en scène is not quite the same.

In " La Mort de Tintagiles," however, we have something rather different in form and in motive. It is a very simple and affecting little play, although less theoretically consistent with M. Maeterlinck's dramaturgy than others. The child in the grip of the dark and powerful queen, the devoted sisters, their watch and their failure, Ygraine's desperation and revolt,—these are

almost too typical, too symbolic. To present a
symbol is nothing new, even when done with consummate sensitiveness and mastery of feeling; it
is a language not unlike the metaphors of every
day. What M. Maeterlinck seemed to be feeling
for was the suggestion of much by means of little
or even nothing. And in spite of the beauty of
this little piece, I cannot feel in it the elusiveness
that I have thought it M. Maeterlinck's design to
convey. Of the other plays " Intérieur " is not
unlike " L'Intrus " in its general character, and
" Sœur Béatrice " is rather after the fashion of
some other things. I will confess honestly that I
have quite failed, however, to get at it, except so
far as the obvious exoteric proceedings are concerned. But I believe we need not pause on these
plays, for there are others more important.

" Ariane et Barbe Bleue " is a significant little
piece because it is a sort of commentary. There
are castles and caverns as in the other plays, but
at the moment that M. Maeterlinck diverges from
the nursery tale we see at a flash much. When
Ariane looks at the keys which Bluebeard has
given her, and at once selects the forbidden key,
with the calm " That is the only one of value,"
one can see at once, not allegory, not symbolism,
but that M. Maeterlinck throughout is assured
that in prospecting for truth it is useless to go

where people have gone before and found nothing.
He searches in those very places which are forbidden by convention, or authority, or fear of ridi-
cule, or hope of praise, just because the things
which were allowed to all have been explored by all,
to no great effect so far as his own interests were
concerned. That which is permitted is of no value;
it will only distract one's attention. If one regards
the prohibitions of the world, one will go no further than the world. So Ariane at once makes
for the forbidden door. Her nurse opens various
other doors that are not forbidden and finds heaps
of diamonds, pearls, rubies, and other trivial
things. But Ariane opens the forbidden door
and finds—all M. Maeterlinck's heroines. She
finds them in a dark cavern which she makes light
by letting in the sun. They are dazzled at first.
When they can see, they long to go to the woods,
the fields, the ocean. They look upon each other,
and when they see each other as they are they
think it very strange. Still, when they gather in
the hall of the jewels and Bluebeard is delivered to
them, they cannot make up their minds to break
their bonds. They care for him till he returns
to consciousness. Then Ariane says that she
must go away. Nor will she ever come back. One
after another: Mélisande, Sélysette, Ygraine, Bel-
langère, Alladine refuse to accompany her, and

she goes forth alone, leaving them in the hall of jewels.

Somehow one cannot take all that seriously, but in spite of the humour that cannot be denied (indeed it should surely be appreciated) there is something well worth having. *Ex oris infantium;* children have not the wisdom of us elder folks, of course. But we do not deny the frequent value of their clearsightedness. I confess that M. Maeterlinck's long-haired ladies had appeared to me not wholly in keeping with the Treasure of the Humble, Wisdom and Destiny, the Buried Temple. When I read " Ariane et Barbe Bleue " I began to see a glimmering of light on the dark river.

When you begin on " Monna Vanna " you are all at sea again. Here is no symbolism, certainly, whatever there be elsewhere, and no realism either. " Monna Vanna " is not conceived for the static theatre, nor for the romantic theatre that we have become accustomed to. It is a play of the Italian Renaissance, and in externals might be by anybody. If it were by anybody else, one could read it easily enough; but being by M. Maeterlinck, we feel that there must be more than meets the eye.

The first accustomed figure in a world of ordinary strangers is the old man Marco. He has the air of calm wisdom with which we are familiar from M. Maeterlinck's philosophical writings; he is representative of eternal justice; if not of common sense, yet of that sense wherein we " see into the life of things " and which greets us so often if not in M. Maeterlinck's plays, at least in his philosophy. We recognise it and respond to it. In this play, however, his wisdom is not generally recognised; it is indeed intensely irritating to others on the stage. Marco brings to the captain of beleaguered Pisa the offer of the Florentine besieger; let his wife, Monna Vanna, go to the tent of the conqueror in mantle and sandals only, and the town shall be spared. Guido is outraged; Marco imperturbable. " Why do you consider if you have the right to deliver a whole people to death in order to delay for a few hours an evil which is inevitable; for when the city is taken Vanna will fall into the power of the conqueror." The Maeterlinckian wisdom is not understood, save by Vanna herself, who immediately accepts the offer. Guido is indignant and outraged and we certainly must sympathise with him, but how much less wise he is than the other.

When Monna Vanna comes to the tent of Prinzivalle she learns that they have met before; he met her as a child and has loved her for twenty years during all the rush and change of a captain of condottieri. There is something noble in such devotion and Vanna receives it at its true worth.

It is something different from everyday sentiment and feelings. They return together to Pisa.

When they get there it is not remarkable that Guido does not appreciate this noble love as his wife has done. Guido is of the world and cannot understand that people will not do as seems most natural to him. Marco alone appreciates; for the rest no effort can make a really fine piece of Quixotic idealism seem for a moment possible. Those who want to live at a higher level must be satisfied with very few companions.

But I believe M. Maeterlinck succeeds in putting us on his side. Real justice appears beautiful in Marco; real morality in Vanna; real love in Prinzivalle. Such people will understand each other even if everybody else holds them worse than fools or knaves.

The best commentator on M. Maeterlinck, or at least the keenest, is M. Maeterlinck himself. "Joyzelle" is full of explanation. For the moment we may neglect its dramatic character and take it for criticism. Merlin has gained power because he has found Arielle, he has " realised his interior force, the forgotten power that slumbers in every soul." This is the main thing; it is not the common, everyday intellect, will, emotion that will give us an apprehension of a reality that stands all tests; it is something that we are con-

scious of in silence as in " The Treasure of the
Humble," in ecstasy as in " Pélléas et Mélisande,"
in wisdom and justice as in " Monna Vanna." To
those who do not know, Merlin is a bad magician,
just as Marco is a heartless philosopher; but he
has only " done a little sooner what they will do
later," for the age is on the dawn of a spiritual
enlightenment. The world waits for clear day;
a few young men now dream dreams, a few old men
see visions, but the time is approaching when the
clouds shall lift that now hang within a little of
the horizon. In the play Merlin waits for his son
who is to attain by love; who will achieve more
than his father just because he is to win by love
what the other has gained by knowledge. Joyzelle is love, unalloyed, incorruptible, perfect.
She denies everything that contradicts her intuition; like Ariane she perceives that the very for-
bidding of anything renders it necessary; like
Monna Vanna she scruples at no trial. Unlike
most people she cannot be influenced by something that has no relation to her.

This is the enforcement of M. Maeterlinck's
fundamental idea; the laws of life are not to be
deduced from the apparent circumstances of life;
they are to be appreciated by intuition; they are
therefore best known, not by words, by deeds, by
that which can be seen and heard, but in silence,

not actively but passively. Such communication
with the absolute gives one a certain kind of disposition of which the motive power is love and the
directing power wisdom, but of these the latter is
the servant of the former.

Such is an abstract statement of the ideas which
are at the bottom of M. Maeterlinck's work.
They are fundamental conceptions, however, and
on them is based a dramatic art which does not
seem to have varied very much from the original
statement. In " The Double Garden " he gives
us a more recent view in commenting on the drama
of the present. The action is still unimportant.
He does not still insist on the principle that there
should be no external action, but the particular
acts are not of importance. Pélléas may love his
brother's wife, Monna Vanna may go to the tent
of a victorious mercenary, Joyzelle may emulate
Judith,—certainly all the events have the same
character, perhaps but a Gallic accident,—but
in themselves the acts are entirely indifferent and
might be something else. The dialogue is still
simple. It does not continue the effort at realism
which people used to think so funny, but it still
aims to suggest rather than to state. It carries
on the action, but its true purpose is to dissemi-
nate communication of a super-essential character.
In fact the whole aim is to attune the modern mind

to an appreciation of the mystical, to get it to be direct and to disregard circumstance.

A good deal in M. Maeterlinck's dramas has been held to be symbolic. I cannot attach much importance to the opinion. A symbol is not an effective mode of expression. Unless a symbol in long process of time, or otherwise, has attached itself to our emotional life it is rarely of much importance. The hearth, the flag, the cross, these doubtless are symbols, and of immense power, and further they are symbols having what is practically accidental connection with the thing they symbolise. Hearths are sadly uncommon nowadays, flags present either a fancy or a convention of a forgotten heraldry, and the cross is an immense power even when its historic character is forgotten. These symbols have power over us, it is true, but chiefly because their extraordinary and universal acceptance has associated them inextricably with our moral nature. The symbols of men of letters rarely have this power unless there be some real likeness at bottom, as in the conception of a progress from this world to the world to come. Where there is no such reality the symbol is fanciful and has little lasting power. The symbols of Hawthorne, the scarlet letter, Zenobia's flower, have meaning only by the moral vitality which they express.

A symbol, if it be nothing but a symbol, merely serves to mystify, to obscure. Arthur Rimbaud's idea that *A* symbolised blue (or whatever colour it was) and the other vowels, other colours, would obscure matters if any one paid any attention to it, because, although people do attach conceptions of colour to sounds or letters, they differ very greatly about it, so that symbolism of that sort is not expressive, but obscuring. M. Maeterlinck has no desire to be obscure: in his essays he tries to state very simply and directly his ideas on a very inexpressible matter. I remember no symbols properly so called in his philosophical writings, though there are figures for the moment here and there.

The figures and circumstances in his plays, with a few exceptions, are not symbolic; they are examples, types, concrete cases, which are things very different from symbols. They have reality, they have a real marvellousness, to use his quotation from Reaumer, instead of a marvellousness that is changeful and imaginary. M. Maeterlinck himself says that he has long ceased to find in this world any marvel more interesting or more beautiful than truth, or at least than man's effort to know it. And so in his book " Les Abeilles," although there is the constant idea in mind that in the hive we have a form of life that may give

us some knowledge of human life, there is nowhere
any fancy as we may call it, but wherever an
analogy is perceived it is presented very simply
and with abundant explanation and limitation.
" Let us not hasten to draw from these facts con-
clusions as to the life of man." Yet there is
throughout that singularly interesting book the
constant feeling of an analogy that is rarely expressed. The bees act under the impulsion of a
power external to themselves, it would seem, to
which we cannot give a better name than the spirit
of the hive. They are aware of this spirit and
they obey it: but it does not appear that they
know it intellectually or obey it consciously. M.
Maeterlinck's representative figures are like the
bees, they are unconsciously under the domination
of the spirit of the race, of the destiny of humanity, of the wisdom of life. The feeling leads them
to strange acts, it is true, but it does lead them.
Maeterlinck presents them to us and that in a
form in which we may sympathise with them.
That is his work as a dramatist. It is not his
business to preach either by symbol or sermon.
He is content to present the essential things of
life as he recognises them. He presents them in
forms in which, as nearly as may be, those things
which cannot be spoken can be made evident.

So much would seem to apply pretty well to

M. Maeterlinck's earlier work, and indeed to some
of his maturer work. But when we come to apply
it to his latest play and his greatest theatrical
success, it would seem to be written about somebody else. "The Blue Bird" was Maeterlinck's
only production (except translation or adaptation) for five years. It was, however, a more wonderful success than all his other performances put
together. It was a rapturously delightful performance.

What was the cause of this rapture, this
delight? Tyltyl and Mytil, children of a poor
woodcutter, are wakeful on Christmas Eve: they
jump out of bed, climb up on a stool, and look
out of the window at the party of rich children
opposite. The little boy takes all the room at
the window, and allows his sister but a grudging
little place as they wonder at the carriages, the
Christmas-tree, the boys, the cake. Listen to some
scraps of their conversation. The little girl asks
her brother:

" Why don't they eat them at once?
Because they're not hungry.
Not hungry? . . . Why not?
Well, they eat whenever they want to . . .
Every day?
They say so.

Will they eat them all? . . . Will they give
any away?

To whom?

To us . . .

They don't know us . . .

Suppose we asked them . . .

We mustn't . . .

Why not?

Because it's not right."

There surely is the familiar mystery of Maeterlinck. There is more there than meets the eye, if,
somehow, our philosophy could find it out. There
is the insignificant dialogue yet so strangely significant. These two children, so natural, they are
not symbols, as we were just saying, yet they are
representative figures, they are filled with the spirit
which fills men and women, not one, but millions.
The little boy says to his sister, " You are taking
all the room," when the little girl has no room at
all: he finally gives her a miserly small place on the
stool, saying, " Now you're better off than I."
That certainly has a familiar ring. As they look
at the rich children at supper and pretend to have
the cakes they only see, Mytil, the little girl, cries
with delight, " I've got twelve," and her brother
cries, " And I four times twelve ! . . . But I'll
give you some." All that is natural enough, even

realistic enough, but still " significant," as one keeps saying. It reminds one of Maeterlinck's interest in the feminist movement, in his presentation in " Ariane et Barbe Bleue " of the present stimulating question of the relations of men and women, of the gradual development of his heroines from the little oppressed Princesse Maleine to the bighearted deliverer, Monna Vanna.

All that is precisely the Maeterlinck we know. But in a minute there enters the Fairy Bérylune: she wishes to have the Blue Bird for her little girl and sends the children on a search for it. What is the Blue Bird, and why should her little girl want it? Why, the Blue Bird is the unattainable, the great secret of all things, the secret of happiness. The children seek it through many strange regions, through the regions of the dead and the regions of those who are yet to live, through the kingdom of Night and through the Forest where they can see into the lives of Trees and Animals, they seek it through many strange adventures and return without it to their own little cottage to find it singing in the cage in their own little room. They had thought that this was the Blue Bird before, but it had not seemed blue enough.

Now certainly all that is symbolic enough. The children stand for the human race. The Blue Bird is happiness. Man seeks for happiness by all

strange, romantic, wonderful ways and finds it
only in the accustomed familiarities of his own
home and his own heart. And we have further
symbolism. The children at the beginning are
given a diamond which allows them to see into the
souls of things, by which is mystically rendered
the idea that it is through a real science, a science
which gives us the real nature of things in place
of dry classifications, that man will more and more
attain his end. The children are guided in their
search by Light, by which is signified, let us say,
whatever illumination gives one to know the true
nature of things and stimulates further one's desire
to know. This is certainly symbolism, and that of
the simplest and most conventional sort, and we
may add that the ideas are simple and conventional
also. Suppose Maeterlinck at the beginning of
his career had presented merely such ideas as that
all seek abroad for a happiness they finally find at
home, and that illumination, knowledge, science is
the great means by which man is to obtain the
summum bonum: he would not have aroused great
attention nor have attracted much attention to his
message. In fact, so far as its general symbolism
is concerned, " The Blue Bird " only gives its
readers or audiences the pleasure which we find in
running over an old fable told once more in some
new and charming form.

It does not appear, however, that Maeterlinck
attached serious importance to his fable, or if we
choose, to the symbolism of his main idea. He
makes no effort to carry out the allegory systematically. Bunyan in his allegory of the spiritual life is at great pains to have everything bear a
significance which shall help impress his general
idea. He gives first the general analogy of his
figure: Man passes from the worldly life, by the
way of baptism, and through the many trials and
struggles and compensations of the Christian life,
to the heavenly city. And all sorts of details are
harmonious with the general significance and
typify the encouragements and discouragements
of that life, the Interpreter's House, the conflict
with Apollyon, the persecution of Vanity Fair,
Giant Despair. Of course there are certain dis-
crepancies, but they are slight: on the whole, the
analogy is very carefully preserved. But Maeterlinck would seem to have no such care: he can
hardly have meant to indicate that man in his
search for happiness has first sought him in the
regions of remembrance of the dead, and next in
the darkness of ignorance and superstition, and
next in the regions of the life that is yet to come.
The Land of Memory, the Palace of Night, the
Kingdom of the Future, these places have nothing
to do with the search for happiness; they are

merely the embodiment of ideas or fancies that
Maeterlinck happened to have, which he might just
as well have introduced into some entirely different
play. So the striking scene in the churchyard has
no symbolic meaning in relation to the whole: the
Fairy Bérylune sends word that one of the dead
in the churchyard is hiding the Blue Bird in his
tomb; the children go to the graveyard to wait
for the dead to rise at midnight, and as the clock
sounds and the opening graves are seen to be full
of beauty, fragrance, loveliness, they learn that
there are no dead. We may amuse ourselves by
fancying an analogy (one or two have occurred
to me), but certainly none is obvious. This scene,
like the others, is charming and has its own significance, but as far as the rest of the play is concerned it has no more relevance than one of the
incongruous phases of a dream. We learn, for instance, that there are no dead, that the dead live
only in our memory of them. But it appears that
there is an ante-natal life which is very interesting.
So, if we are to imagine the symbolism to be consistent, it would seem that the idea was that life
proceeds to the fine flower of life on this earth and
then stops. But such consistency was no part
of the author's idea. In a very general way
only does he present ideas that he deems interesting
and important.

This lack of meaning as a whole and of structure interferes to my mind with the pleasure we get from reading or from seeing the play. We get no general impression from it, except, as Lowell said of Emerson, the impression that something beautiful has passed our way, and we remember many phases of the beautiful vision. But if there is any real, psychological value in dramatic unity and structure, if the artistic development of an idea can really give more pleasurable emotion than no development, if a good plot is more interesting than no plot at all, then we do not get from " The Blue Bird " that particular kind of pleasure that a well-constructed play can give. We get other pleasures that are well worth while: for instance, the characterisation is full of real and unexpected excellence. The Dog is the great masterpiece of the play, but he is not the only one. The different characteristics of the children, of the things, are almost as good. Bread, for instance, the perfect type of self-sufficient commonplace domesticity; although it must be confessed that, save in one instance, he is not of the actual use to the children that bread is to man. Then the ingenuity of the especial incidents and ideas: the Sicknesses in the cave of Night, grown weak and feeble at the assaults of man, especially since the germ-theory; the conspiracy of the Trees and Animals against man failing at the first production of steel. These things are a constant source of pleasure throughout the play. Also it would not be Maeterlinck, if the unimportant words and phrases spoken by the way were not in reality the truly significant ones. Take, for instance, the answer of Tyltyl, which might be the watchword of Science, " I must see everything . . . Light said so." Or Granny Tyl's affectionate, " Why, nothing's different when we're able to kiss each other."

So, too, the underlying idea of the transformation of the animals and elements and things that accompany the children, that it is by an appreciation of the true souls of things that man will be helped in his age-long search for the secret of happiness. That is Maeterlinck all over, and especially that it is by a comprehension of the true nature of the simple surroundings of daily life, the dog and the cat, milk and sugar, water and fire, that it is by a true knowledge of real life that one will be aided in one's search for the *summum bonum*. Here, too, however, it will not be malevolent to suggest that though the idea is one which has many applications to life, yet the particular development in the play does not indicate anything, for the souls of animals, elements, things, when the children have got to know them, are not of any great aid to them upon their search.

With all this detraction (which seems very mean
and petty when one re-reads the book), " The Blue
Bird " was a very great achievement. Written
ostensibly for children, it charmed great audiences
wherever it was presented. It was such an opportunity for spectacular display that stage managers and scenic artists were able to develop most
beautiful effects and elaborate combinations. It
was in itself (without any thought of symbol or
significance) so pleasing and amusing as it went
along with its constant whim and fancy, and its
suggestion of things more serious, that all other
considerations seemed of minor importance. It was
so evidently a play of thought, and very " modern " at that, with its placid denial of our fundamental ideas of morality and religion and its thorough recognition of the scientific attitude. It was
pre-eminently a popular piece, and yet it was perfectly characteristic of its author. A wonderful
change had been wrought since " Princesse Maleine."

But " The Blue Bird " has been but one (if the
most important) of the indications of Maeterlinck's assured and definite position in the world
of ideas and of art. He has published somewhat
in prose, as always, in the form of essays now more
self-conscious than the earlier simple statements
of belief and less interesting in content. He has

been criticised and commented upon by others in the form of many newspaper and magazine articles and of essays like the present. But most interesting of all comments have been those made by the rendering by great artists of his conceptions into the forms of a companion art. In 1902 the music of M. Debussy for " Pélléas et Mélisande " was produced: in 1907 the rendering by M. Dukas of " Ariane et Barbe Bleue," in 1910 the setting of " Monna Vanna " by M. Fevrier. In each case it would be quite wrong to say the play was set to music, for that would seem to make the music merely an assistant art. Nor would it be right, either, to say that the composer took the play for a libretto, for that (in our usual view of things) would seem to make the poetry merely a means for the music. Rather should we say that in these operas is realised the Wagnerian ideal of the different arts co-operating each as complement of the other. Doubtless even here there would be difference of opinion. There are those who will see chiefly in " Ariane et Barbe Bleue " a pronunciamento in favour of the rights of woman. Bluebeard will represent the tyranny and oppression of man, and Ariane will be the clear-sighted woman of to-day, who while leaving her foolish sisters behind in her struggle for self-realisation, is thereby more than ever fascinating to the brutal and sub-

dued old tyrant. Others, however, will neglect
such obvious significances and will find the composer to be " the true poet, the only poet in the
deep sense of the word, he who has created ' Ariane
et Barbe Bleue,' " and will find in the music the
highest revelation of a spiritual meaning which
far transcends any practical or political application to conditions of the moment. We need not
decide between the two, certainly not in these
pages. We may see in the two interpretations
the largeness of Maeterlinck's ideas. They are
broad enough to fit many a practical case : they
are lofty enough to offer plenty of superphysical
significance.

Another of Maeterlinck's pieces that was intended for music has lately come upon the stage
in another way. This is the miracle play called
" Sister Beatrice." This play was written some
time ago for music announced as being composed
by M. Gilkas, but I have seen no account of its
operatic production. There are passages in the
play, however, which seem to have been undoubtedly intended for musical expression. Indeed, the
whole piece, like " Ariane et Barbe Bleue," is one
which makes a musical appeal, as one might say,
that is, its meaning is not to be expressed simply
in such and such words, it is not an appeal simply
to a literary appreciation, but like Maeterlinck's

earlier poetry, to a larger nature. The play is founded on an old cloister-legend of the sister who leaves the convent with her lover, and returns after a long and hard experience to find that the Virgin has taken her place during the years in the world of life; but the particular form of the play amounts to little, and, indeed, is left vague and indeterminate. It is but the body: Maeterlinck's real interest here is with the spirit. And the spirit, the whole sentiment—the difference between sacred and profane love—that is such that one feels here more even than elsewhere the need of music or something of the sort. In a measure that need is filled by stage production, even without music, just how successfully many can judge who have lately seen it.

Maeterlinck's latest play is " Marie Magdalene." Here he has by no means attained the stage success of " The Blue Bird," and yet as one reads the book one feels more of the old Maeterlinck there than in anything since " Monna Vanna." The play is most simple and even untheatrical, appealing in its best elements to the reader rather than to the audience. A few years ago another play on the same subject was translated from the German of Paul Heyse, and presented by the most gifted actress of our stage. A mere glance of comparison with Maeterlinck's play shows that though much less interesting to read, it would be more interesting to see. Heyse was interested in the situation of three persons, Judas and Flavius the lovers, and Mary called from her life of earthly loves by the voice of Christ. The play is full of people of definite characters, all having something to do. In Maeterlinck's play it is not so: the action is of the simplest. Indeed the interest seems hardly in the action at all (how should it be with Maeterlinck?), but rather with the soul of Mary. And here certainly Maeterlinck has had remarkable success. That strange incomprehensible conversion to another life that no one still in the old life can understand, Maeterlinck gives us something of an idea of. Indeed, it is rather curious that Maeterlinck and Bernard Shaw (in "Major Barbara"), neither of whom poses as a very ardent follower of the Christian faith, should have been able to express the spirit of the Christian life so much better than many others, who would seem on the face of it so much better fitted. However that be, Maeterlinck was interested in presenting in Mary a certain disposition, and that he has done wonderfully well. Whoever wants to know something of that state of soul may read the play and find it. He will find other things, too, though perhaps not very effective on the stage, nor such as we can easily or rightly value there. Maeterlinck has gathered together so much of what is familiar to us in the Gospel; the Beatitudes, the words to the woman taken in adultery, the crowds of lame, halt, and blind, as well as those possessed by devils, the raising of Lazarus, the anointing of Jesus by the woman who was a sinner; there is so much in all that, that in itself cannot fail to affect us, that it is hard to say how much is the power of M. Maeterlinck. Chiefly his own, however, is certainly the Roman philosopher: he is not so truly learned as the philosophers of M. Anatole France, but he presents a certain rational philosophy with which the readers of Maeterlinck are already familiar. He is a worthy successor of those other wise old men whom we remember, Arkel in "Pélléas et Mélisande," Marco in "Monna Vanna." But after all, the chief interest is in Mary. Doubtless it is not a very accurate rendering or reconstruction: but what reason is there for supposing that the real Mary of Magdala was a person of any such life or character as that to which tradition has condemned her? Not very true to fact, probably, but a real disposition, hers, the disposition of one who somehow has been rescued from the turning treadmill that we call the world, and simply cannot understand the possibility of going back there again. That is the chief thing about Maeterlinck: he seems (at times) to have the idea of a different kind of life from that which we know, a transcendental life. As he presents it, it has a charm that makes us wish to know it too, and any one who does so wish may make some acquaintance with it in this latest play of his.

OUR IDEA OF TRAGEDY

Some years ago Mr. Courtney delivered three lectures at the Royal Institution which he published under the title, " The Idea of Tragedy." So far as offering any explanation of the power of tragedy in this world, he was not very successful. The essence of tragedy, thought Mr. Courtney, lay in the conflict presented. But every one knows that conflict in itself is not tragic: as commonly thought of, conflict may be tragic and may not. Mr. Courtney spoke of the Attic tragedy as presenting the conflict of the human will against fate, of Shakespearean tragedy as presenting the conflict of the human will with the laws that guide the universe. When he got to modern times, however, his courage failed him: " The Second Mrs. Tanqueray " was his ideal, and he saw very clearly that there was no conflict there to make tragedy. So he abandoned his idea and took a new one: inspired by Ibsen, he added that in modern tragedy the main idea is failure to achieve one's mission.

The first of these ideas was by no means new. It will be found in many places in æsthetic literature.   Let me quote a statement of it not so common as some others: it has in it some very interesting criticism of poetry:

> " Say what meant the woes
> By Tantalus entailed upon his race,
> And the dark sorrows of the line of Thebes?
> Fictions in form, but in their substance truth,
> Tremendous truths! familiar to the men
> Of long-past times, nor obsolete in ours.
> Exchange the shepherd's frock of native grey
> For robes with regal purple fringed; convert
> The crook into a sceptre; give the pomp
> Of circumstance, and here the tragic Muse
> Shall find apt subjects for her highest art.
> Amid the groves, under the shadowy hills,
> The generations are prepared; the pangs,
> The internal pangs are ready; the dread strife
> Of poor humanity's afflicted will
> Struggling in vain with ruthless destiny."

In that passage Wordsworth expresses his idea in almost exactly the words of Mr. Courtney, and says, too, that this conflict between will and fate, the subject of Greek tragedy, is still a power ready to the hand of the poet of the day.

The other notion of tragedy, too, may be found in the poetry of our day, notably in that of

Browning, whose tragedy, when he presents us with tragedy, generally consists, not so much in strife, as in failure to do that which was possible, that which one's best nature demanded. It is of this form of tragedy he writes in the " Lost Leader," where Wordsworth served him as example as he has served me with precept.

But all this seems to me a little superficial. Granted that tragedy consists sometimes of a conflict, a strife, whether between the human will and fate, or between humanity and natural law; sometimes of a failure to fulfil one's mission, to be what one might be, to " live one's own life," according to the phrase of the day or the day before yesterday,—it is still a question why these matters should affect us as tragedy does affect us. That is my interest: literature or art, tragedy or any other element in it is vitally important to us, only as it affects, touches, moves us. And any theory of tragedy, to take any real part in our thinking and feeling, must make clearer to us why we are moved, or how, in order that we may appreciate, in the tragedies that we see, the things that are really strong and true.

It may first, however, be a matter of interest to some unsophisticated souls who have no theory on the subject, and have often enjoyed tragedies keenly without any, to know why we should wish

to discuss the idea of tragedy in the drama of our
day.   Why the idea of tragedy rather than the
idea of farce or of comedy or any other idea?
Or even why talk of such abstractions at all?

Let me explain why nobody should be without a
theory of tragedy.   I may add that I have already
presented the matter to the public, to the acceptance, unfortunately, of no one that I ever heard
of, and to the utter rejection of one competent
authority on the drama.   If I do not endeavour
to controvert the opinions of this latter learned
critic, it is not because I do not respect them.   It
is because the spectacle of two academic theorists
disputing on the matter of tragedy—two budge
doctors of the Stoic fur disputing over the fit of
a buskin—would be inharmoniously humorous.
So I must bid her farewell (ave atque vale!), my
fair theorist with her " tragic blame " and so
forth.   I shall never convert her—perhaps no one
else—but I shall enjoy tragedy all the same in my
own way, more, I hope, than it is possible to do in
hers.

We may well enough discuss the idea of tragedy
in the drama of our day, or of any other, because
by the pretty general consent of mankind, or that
part of it that cares for letters, tragedy is regarded as the highest and noblest literary form.
A great tragedy stands higher in the estimation

of the world than a great lyric or a great novel.
Aristotle considered tragedy the crowning achievement of the human intellect, though the Greeks
in general gave the first place to Homer.   The
English world considers Shakespeare the greatest
author of all times, though Keats thought that the
epic was the truly great form and Poe the lyric.
These are differences of opinion and the question
is not very important: some of the world's masterpieces are tragedies and some are not.   In the
drama, however, tragedy easily holds the most important place.   We like to laugh at a farce, to be
thrilled at a melodrama, to be charmed at a
comedy,—and we may not like a tragedy as much
as these things.   But generally people admit that
it is greater.   It may be too great for us at some
given time,—there will be plenty of evenings when
we had rather go to some bright comedy or some
exciting melodrama, or even to the vaudeville or
the music hall, if it comes to that, as it often does,
—than to any tragedy ever written.   But that is
just as we do not always want to read the very
best literature, do not always want to be hearing
classic music, do not always want to be looking
at the Sistine Madonna, say; do not always want
to wear our best clothes and sit in the parlour.
We acknowledge pretty generally that tragedy is
the great thing, though we may not be always in

the mood for it.   Few persons of taste can experience profoundly the emotion of a great tragedy and hold that any other dramatic form is equally great.

This theoretic view we might present on the basis of current facts.   That is, practically all the great plays of which we have been speaking are tragedies.   We may not feel quite sure just what is conveyed by the term tragedy, but we can generally tell one when we see it, if only by the simple fact that the chief figure dies at the end, or at least comes to an end in the particular world in which we know him, which is much the same thing. There is nothing essentially noble in death, I suppose, nor is death on the stage always tragic, but we do have this particular ending in " Cyrano " and " L'Aiglon," in " Die versunkene Glocke " and " Es lebe das Leben," in " The Second Mrs. Tanqueray," in " Pélléas et Mélisande," though not in " Candida," presumably.

And if the greatest of our modern plays have the same purpose as the greatest plays of the old Athenian days, of the great Elizabethan time, of the French classic period ; why, it is worth our while to spend a time in studying out their essential characteristic, if it be only that we may be sure to gain from these plays the highest form of pleasure, that we do not get too much interested in minor matters, but find out in them what is best.

For it is well to remark that there is no especial importance in the abstract definition of the term " tragedy " or of any other term in æsthetics. That is in itself a matter of slight moment for us. There is, it is true, intense pleasure in speculating on æsthetic subjects for those who like it (as I do), just as there is intense pleasure in speculating over any other point in psychology, or any other science. But that is something for the lover of speculation, not for the lover of literature: it has, as such, no more to do with the appreciation of the drama than any other kind of speculation. Many people have an intuitive delight at fine things on the stage, which is far more intense than the reasoned pleasure of a cut-and-dried critic. It is not for the importance of the definition that it is worth while to go over the subject.

No, it is for a more practical reason. It is that we may have a notion of the true sources of pleasure, or, rather, of the sources of the truest pleasure. A dozen people will go to the same play and enjoy a dozen different things. One had eyes for the costumes, another for the stage-settings, another was carried away by the sweet smile of the actress, another got " a great moral lesson " (I suppose there must be such people, or the matter

would not figure in the advertisements), another
was delighted at the careful dramatic construction, another enjoyed the fine delivery of the poet's
lines (that couldn't have been in America, unless
perhaps it was the Chorus in " Henry V."), another was immensely impressed somehow in a way
he could not explain. If we are one of these and
talk to some of the others, and find that we have
really missed something worth while,—or, to put
it more simply, if we find, on reading a criticism
the next morning, that there was more than met
our eye,—why, then we may feel as though
we had not got from the play all that was there.
And if we go again we shall perhaps aim to get
the true thrill, and look out especially for it.
Our friend who said of " Cyrano de Bergerac "
that " The most popular play of the final decade
of the century presents no problem whatever, and
avoids any criticism of life," was one who looked
in " Cyrano " for problems and criticism of life,
because he thought that a great play ought to
have those things. A problem, in the sense in
which people say that Pinero deals with problems,
" Cyrano " has not, and a good thing, too. And
as for a criticism of life, it certainly does not have
that in potted form. Those things it does not
have; what it does have is better worth while than
either. But the point is that such a critic does

not get from " Cyrano " even that which it has,
because he looks for something it had not, which,
to his mind, was the real thing.

Now with tragedy it is commonly supposed that
there is something especial about it which influences all men; that human nature is such as to be
susceptible to this something, which appears in all
sorts of forms, always different, but always having upon the souls of men the same moving effect.
Just what this something is, the critics have found
it hard to say. Just what is the moving effect
that it has, has been occasion of various explanation. But it is the pretty general opinion that in
all tragedy there is a single something, and that
people are and have been affected by it in much
the same way. It is not necessary that this
should be the case. The Athenians were very different from us. It might be that there were
things about their tragedies that have no especial
effect upon us, and that we enjoy things to which
they paid small attention. With the Elizabethan
drama there is no doubt of the matter; Shakespeare's audiences cared greatly for things which
are even distasteful to us, and we enjoy things
which they hardly noticed. But these things are
minor matters; the real tragedy is the same to-day
that it was in Shakespeare's day, that it was in
the time of the Greeks. If, then, we see some

great and common quality in all great tragedy,
if we see some great and common quality in human
nature now and two thousand years ago, and if
the common quality of great tragedy seems to
bear some relation to the quality of human nature,
far more if it seem to be a natural cause of it, —
why, then we may well believe that the success of
a great tragedy, the existence in it of a lasting
appeal to mankind, comes not from accident nor
from art, but from the presence of the truly
tragic quality which moved the Athenians in the
days when Æschylus presented " Prometheus
Bound," which was felt when " Hamlet " was just
put on the stage, just as it is felt to-day in not
a few pieces which for minor reasons we cannot
compare with those masterpieces of the human
mind.

To talk over this question is to attune ourselves
to it.   It is not a matter of definition which one
may read in a book and learn by heart.   It is a
matter of looking into one thing or another and
trying to feel keenly what is there.   It is doubtless the case that some people feel artistic beauty
keenly with no sense of why or wherefore, and it
is probably the case also that other people feel
artistic beauty, just as keenly but in a somewhat
different way, with more consciousness of causes
and reasons.   Both kinds of enjoyment are good

if both be intense and genuine. A person who enjoys keenly, with no idea of why, has usually more artistic appreciation than the person who thinks much or reasons. But both may enjoy more keenly by training, or, in this case, by talking or thinking over the matters in question and discussing the characteristics that are of interest.

The first and simplest idea of tragedy is of a play with an unhappy ending. That is not very abstruse, but it is characteristic of all tragedies— Greek, Elizabethan, French, modern—what more would you have?

Why, this much more, a knowledge of why an unhappy ending should be pleasing to us, why we should think it delightful to see an unhappy ending,—in fact, whether every unhappy ending is pleasing to us,—why any one should call the writing of a play with an unhappy ending the top achievement of the human intellect? In other words, is not this unhappy ending something necessary to tragedy, perhaps, but not the essential characteristic? In logic a quality always to be found, and yet not essential, is called an inseparable accident. For instance, it is in England an inseparable accident with a clergyman that he wears a white tie, and yet this costume has no essential connection with his holy calling. Perhaps the true and essential tragic quality necessitates an unhappy ending as far as the chief character is concerned, and yet that unhappy ending is not itself the essentially tragic thing. In fact this is almost necessarily the case, for in a tragedy we feel the tragic quality long before the end, and therefore it cannot be the end only that has the tragic quality.

And, even if it could rationally be the case, the unhappiness of the end would hardly be a sufficient explanation, for we should still want to know why the end seemed to us unhappy. A tragic ending is often the death of the hero. But death is not necessarily unhappy—in a large way, that is. To those immediately concerned it is always a cause of unhappiness, it is true. But death is a necessity, and we would not, even if we could, avoid it; even M. Metchnikoff agrees to that. It is the natural, the appropriate end of our life here. It is often not tragic at all, but triumphant, glorious. Why is such and such a death unhappy? The word merely begs the question and puts us on a new inquiry no easier than the old.

So those who like to speculate on such matters have thought of other reasons, and a good many other definitions and descriptions of the idea of tragedy have been put forward. I shall not deal with them for many reasons, one of which is that it would take a whole book instead of the tail-end

of one, and another, that it is more amusing to
hear a man talk of what he thinks himself, than of
what other people think.

It is the general opinion—and a very natural
one—that, in trying to determine the nature of
the tragic quality, we must find something which
does not belong to the drama alone. We use the
word " tragic " far too widely to confine ourselves
to anything to be found only in dramatic form.
If it were for no other reason than that the drama
represents life, we might say that whatever is
effective in a large way in the drama will be an
element effective in life as well. But then, also,
we use the word, half figuratively perhaps, but
still broadly. In all forms of literature we have
what we may call tragedy, and in life as well.
Indeed, if we were going into a general theoretical
consideration, we ought to go far beyond the
narrow limits of the drama; all literature, all art
we ought to examine, history, life we ought to consider to find the essential of the tragic quality.

Looking on the matter, without confining ourselves necessarily to literature, tragedy seems to
depend largely upon a sense on our part of in-
soluble mystery or strangeness, in some action or
bit of life that we are viewing. Such a sense
everybody must have very often had in viewing
life, art, literature. Let us consider a case or

two; take the example of Heinrich the Bell-caster,
he whose love of art led him away from his home
to a mountain-top; led him to desert his wife for
a mountain-spirit; led him finally to that point
where his wife sought refuge beneath the waters
of the mountain tarn, while his mountain-spirit
vanished away to the home of the Nickelmann.
Here would be a tragedy entirely aside from Heinrich's dying.   It would be a tragedy surely, even
if he were left alive, because we can see how life
would continue with him.   And why a tragedy?
Can we analyse it?   For one thing, we may note
that we have here a pretty general motive, the
contest between the life of art and the everyday
life of home, the contest that finds expression nowadays in all sorts of forms, notably in d'Annunzio's " Giaconda " and Sudermann's " Heimat,"
or in the figure of Marchbanks in " Candida."
The thing is this: here is Art, the pursuit of the
Beautiful, the care-charmer, the teacher, the great
amuser of mankind, the recuperator of the weary
by ever-changing delight—art is all that, is it
not? a very necessary factor in life, I am sure.
And yet how often does this very necessary factor
jar and collide with and crush that other very
necessary factor, namely, the simple, plain, good
life of the home, of morality, of every day.   And
vice versa.   Is there not an instinctive contrast

between the idea of the artist and the idea of the
father, the citizen, the respectable everyday man?
There certainly is, although we may get over it by
thinking we ought to, and that there should be
any such contrast, that there should be a conflict,
as it were, between these two important elements
in life, that they should seem inharmonious, is
surely, to me at least, a very strange thing, a
matter not yet solved and made plain to us. Hence
pictures of this strife, if they be broad and general, give us the tragic element. If they be well
done they impress us powerfully, because they
thrust us into a region where we are afraid, where
we cannot reckon upon results, where we cannot
answer the pressing questions which come, but
have simply to acknowledge that we do not know.

Not that everything that we do not understand
is tragic. There are many things that we do not
understand at all, although we always behave as
though we did, namely, those things that are a
great joy to us. The nature of love, for instance,
is very imperfectly understood by us, yet happy
love is not tragic, because, though we do not pene-
trate to its depths, it seems all right and precisely
what it should be. It does not seem to us a mystery, it seems very natural and necessary, and, indeed, when we get used to it, an everyday affair.
The normal course of love is like the normal course

of many other things: the question of comprehension, of understanding, simply never comes up in
regard to them, we do not try to understand them,
we see that they work to the advantage of mankind, that they are in harmony with life as we look
at it, that we could not make them better in any
detail, and so, whether we grasp them intellectually or not, we do not trouble ourselves about
them. And yet sometimes even happy love, since
we have spoken of it, has its tragic element. I
spoke a few pages back of Mr. Sothern's presentation of "Romeo and Juliet." One of the most
beautiful moments in the play, and yet the most
pitiful and the most tragic, was that scene at the
Capulet feast, where these two who loved at first
sight first are conscious that they love. It is not
that we know what is about to happen to them
that gives us a thrill. No, it is simply the strange
sight of these two, their souls in their eyes, moving mechanically in the world of masquers, Juliet
in the dance, Romeo by the wall, with life to them
a totally different thing from what it was a moment before. Certainly a very strange conception, and well calculated to stagger any one without great indifference or great confidence in the
order of Nature and in her always proceeding in
the very best way. Still, as a rule, such situations
are not conceived of as tragic.

Another great mass of circumstances is not tragic, even though it presents us with most noteworthy inconsistencies or incongruities. This is where the circumstances are trivial or superficial. Matters of this sort are not tragic, but comic. The foundation of the Ludicrous is often said to be the incongruous, and the incongruous is that which for the moment is inconsistent. And the inconsistent is something that we cannot for the moment harmonise in our thoughts or render comprehensible. The ludicrous often, indeed always, depends upon the point of view. Thus a dignified gentleman walking on the street steps on the ice or upon a piece of orange-peel and falls down. It is very funny to some people, but the man himself rarely perceives the humour of it. It is incongruous, the contrast between his dignity and his lack of dignity. For the moment the mind of the spectator refuses to correlate the ideas. But in a minute the situation becomes perfectly natural; pitiable, but not tragic. Experience steps in and tells us that there is nothing incongrous or inconsistent. And the matter ceases to be ludicrous. If you come home and tell some one that you saw a dignified man fall down upon the ice, you cannot, probably, make it seem funny to anybody else because, although it is incongruous to them as it was to you, so far as the minor aspects of the

matter are concerned, the mind is not taken by
surprise, and regards the matter as one of the
necessary and normal results of winter.

Other cases, however, present more difficulty in
discrimination.   There are not a few cases where
the same thing may seem tragic or humorous.
The classic example, as we may say, is that of
Mr. Shandy and My Uncle Toby.   Here were two
brothers who loved each other devotedly, and yet
were totally unable to understand each other.   As
Sterne handles the situation, fixing attention on
minor points, veiling any deeper feelings that
might have been aroused, it is very purely humorous.   But after all, it is not a humorous situation if dealt with seriously.   Two beings bound
together by close ties, loving each other but never
able to understand each other, something like that
is the situation on which Ibsen built " The Doll's
House."   The same thing may often be comic and
tragic to different people.   The nose of Cyrano
de Bergerac was intensely humorous to many
about him: it was so incongruous that it was
enough to make anybody laugh who could keep
out of the way of the owner.   But to Cyrano himself it was far from humorous, and it shows the
power of the dramatist that he makes us forget
the ridiculous possibilities, so that the figure of
Cyrano is really a noble one.

Incongruity is merely inconsistency, merely that we cannot comprehend two things in one thought.   Incomprehensibleness is at the bottom of tragedy.   We must have something great, something of importance, and then, if the incongruity, the inconsistency, be brought out strongly and poignantly, the thing is done.

One reason for disagreement as to tragic quality is that it often happens that a thing is important to one set of people, but not to another. Then there will be difference of opinion.   For example, the so-called problem-plays of Mr. Pinero. These plays are not great tragedies because they (and their problems) do not make a very wide appeal.   For example, " Iris ": the motive of " Iris " is that of the weak woman who wants to be good but wants more to have an easy, delightful, luxurious, lazy time.   That motive may be capable of tragic force.   Such women may have much charm and beauty of character, so that in easy circumstances they add to the true joy of the world.   Iris was such a one.   She was even more: she was—in ways that did not trouble her—good and generous.   Now, why should such good characteristics all be overbalanced by this one evil? Further, Iris was practically betrayed by her own generosity.   Why should one's doing a good thing lead one inexorably to the doing such wrong

things that one's life is wrecked and other people's
too? There seems to be, then, the possibility of
tragedy there, because that is one of the mysteries
of the human heart and of divine law. But even
were the motive more strongly worked out, the
tragedy would not be a great one because, in the
form in which it comes to us, it is not of wide
application. I suppose I do not know a single
Iris myself, and I question whether the average
man does. I may be able to imagine them readily,
I may be able to judge that there are not a few
of them in certain spheres of life. But the question does not come near enough home to me, or
to most people, for us to call it really tragic. So
of Mrs. Tanqueray, Mrs. Ebbsmith, and the rest
of Mr. Pinero's problematic ladies. They are immensely interesting to themselves and their friends,
no doubt, but only by great art could they be
made so vivid to the world at large as to become
great figures. Alexandre Dumas achieved the
difficult feat when he created Marguerite Gautier, La Dame aux Camélias, commonly called by
us Camille. When I saw the play I was a boy
in college; it is a season when such motives seem
more real than in after years. I remember perfectly well standing up in the back of the theatre
with the tears rolling down my cheeks. In fact
I remember myself much better than I remember

Marguerite Gautier, though I occasionally stimulate my memory by reading the play over. The
fact is that she does not have a universal appeal.

The more important the case, the wider the
appeal, the more certain of success,—other things
being equal,—is the tragedy. It is in this way
that I explain the success of M. Rostand. The
motive of all his plays is the same. It is not very
clearly presented. It is usually conceived in a
spirit that impresses the audience as pessimistic,
but it is always there and always the same and
always the strongest motive in the world. It is
that of the failure of the idealist to attain the
height of his aspiration.

In the " Princesse Lointaine " the imaginative
Rudel loves the ideal princess of Tripoli. He dies
before attaining his ideal, but also before he knows
what his ideal was worth, save as an ideal. In
" Cyrano de Bergerac " we have a man who has,
and who knows that he has,—and we know it too,
—tremendous powers, but who is never able to
realise them, who is never able to appear to the
world as he knows he is. There is that fatal im-
pediment. Purely typical that is, but every one
has something of the sort, for it is inherent in
human nature that the flesh should hold back the
spirit. In his case the spirit of the man is so
fine, he is so brilliant, so vigorous, so courageous,

that he carries it all off with a vitality that makes us almost forget the tragedy. But it is there all the same. In " L'Aiglon " we have the idealist once more, the man who has the greatest ideal of his time, the finest, noblest, most splendid possibility, at least, waiting for him, calling insistently, beckoning, but he cannot ever reach it, chiefly because he cannot even understand what it is. To the Duc de Reichstadt Napoleon was a man of victories and processions and uniforms. He realises as the play goes on that he cannot even in thought rise to the ideal before him, much less realise it in fact. He is noble because he even then clings to his ideal because it is an ideal. A tragic figure he is on the field of Wagram, relapsing into the pathetic when in the last act he becomes, as one might say, more of a child than ever. And this constant defeat of the idealist in this world I take to be a matter not thoroughly understood by us. It is true that the poets offer their explanations, Tennyson with his

> " O me! for why is all around us here
> As if some lesser god had made the world,
> But had not force to shape it as he would,
> Till the High God behold it from beyond,
> And enter it and make it beautiful! "

and Browning with his constant optimism:

" Ah, but a man's reach should exceed his grasp,
Or what's a heaven for? "

But I cannot say that the explanations make it
very clear to me. Still it is the incomprehensible
nature of the thing that makes it striking. It
masters us; if we understood it, we should master
it. If we understood it thoroughly, and saw that
it was just as we should imagine it, or as we
might ourselves have arranged it, or even as we
acknowledge just, then we should not think it anything very much out of the common run. It
would make us cynical, perhaps, or hopeless, but
it would not be the *medicina mentis* that tragedy is.

Such—at any rate let me assume it, for the
time, in spite of conflicts, missions, tragic blames,
and anything else—such is tragedy always, a pur-
suing of some of the strange and unexplainable
courses of life. The finer and nobler the actors,
the greater and more general the evil that they
do not escape, the greater the tragedy. We see
it in the Greek drama, and we see it in the Elizabethan. In the " Prometheus " we have the friend
of man, and therefore one who must endure a life
of torture, as so many friends of man have endured
since his day. In " Hamlet " we have the man in
whom the godlike reason was stronger than in any

other man of his time, and who therefore fell a vic-
tim to an unscrupulous politician. And the same
thing is in modern plays, as we have seen, whether
presented in the beautiful and glittering forms of
romance or in the more immediate forms of everyday life.

There can be little doubt that the element is
there,—may be found, I believe, in every great
tragedy in the drama, literature, in life. But
even if so the real question is: Is it this that thrills
and holds us, when we read the drama or see the
play? Is it this that impresses us with what we
call the Tragic?

To give a sort of answer to this question I must
be a little pedantic. We all know the position of
Aristotle in the intellectual world, how he dominated the thought of man for centuries and is to-
day as wise as ever, though not so dictatorial. He
thought about almost everything in his day and he
did not disdain the drama. He viewed the Athenian drama of his time just as he viewed the
science, the oratory, the politics, the constitutional
principles, and everything else. He analysed its
power and stated it in words that have given the
theorists great opportunities.

" Tragedy," he says, " is an imitation of an
action that is serious, complete, and of a certain
magnitude; in language embellished with every

kind of artistic ornament, the several kinds being found in separate parts of the play; in the form of action not of narrative, through pity and awe effecting the proper *Katharsis* of these emotions."

This word *Katharsis*, it seems generally agreed, was a medical term, meaning much the same thing as our word *purgative*. Tragedy is a purge to the moral nature, it would appear, is the idea of Aristotle. It is an influence upon our moral nature, a purifying, strengthening, reviving influence. It does away with certain evils that annoy our daily life. Its very bitterness—like the purge in " Pilgrim's Progress "—has this effect upon us, and we listen to a tragedy with the same acrid sense of tonic improvement that we feel when we are getting over a cold, say, or an illness. That seems to be Aristotle's view: I take it to be pretty sound. It shows that two thousands years ago he noticed what we may notice to-day.

Certain things in human life have this effect upon us, though they commonly work in rather a drawn-out way, and in art, in so far as art represents life. In tragedy we appreciate Man as Pope thought of him, that much-neglected poet who said so many things so much better than any one else could ever say them. Pope saw the fact, though he had not the artistic feeling to put it in any but an intellectual way:

" Placed on this isthmus of a middle state,
  A being darkly wise and rudely great;
  With too much knowledge for the sceptic side,
  With too much weakness for the stoic's pride,
  He hangs between, in doubt to act or rest,
  In doubt to deem himself a god or beast,
  In doubt his mind or body to prefer,
  Born but to die, and reasoning but to err;
  Alike in ignorance, his reason such,
  Whether he thinks too little or too much;
  Chaos of thought and passion all confused,
  Still by himself abused and disabused;
  Created half to rise and half to fall,
  Great Lord of all things, yet a prey to all.
  Sole judge of truth, in endless error hurled,
  The glory, jest, and riddle of the world!"

The glory to the eye of faith, but the jest to
the comedian and the riddle to those in whom the
spirit is tuned to the note of tragedy.

Or in other words, when we have put before us
one of those poignant scenes, or situations, or moments, or figures of human life, where good and
evil, strength and weakness are so inextricably
mixed, where all that might, that should turn out
so well, does turn out so ill, then we cannot comprehend intellectually, do not try to, we can simply receive the impression emotionally or spiritu-

ally, we cannot but be seized by a mixture of pity
and awe, as Aristotle says. And that feeling is
our feeling for the Tragic.

It leaves us calmed and quieted. Things seem
a little different. Everyday matters at which we
were so hot, for the moment are small and petty.
We feel in a confused way that life is something
fine, big, and noble, and that we ourselves are not
the only people of importance. It does not last,
of course; we shall again be angered, ridiculous,
blunderers, but for the time we are satisfied. We
are willing to continue our lives in their silly individuality, feeling that we may confidently trust
in a power whose detailed purposes have not been
explained to us.

Such in its result is the general effect of the
greatest art. It is of great art that that figure
of the beautiful youth that Emerson mentions is
typical, Phosphorus, whose aspect is such that all
persons who look upon it become silent.

APPENDIX

PERFORMANCE OR PUBLICATION

In the following lists are the dates of the first performance or publication of the plays of our dramatists. They do not pretend to do more than to show the place of each play in the author's career, and to give a general idea of his activity and of public interest in his work. Many matters of curious interest are therefore omitted. This is especially the case with Bernard Shaw and M. Maeterlinck, whose plays have been performed at all sorts of times and places, but not, as a rule, immediately on writing. Performances in countries or languages other than the author's have been noted, but without idea of completeness, to give an idea of the way the author has come before the public. The facts come wherever possible from the published texts of the authors, but in other cases from periodicals, newspapers, dramatic lists, etc.

EDMOND ROSTAND.

(Unless especially mentioned, the place of production was Paris)

1894. May 21. Théâtre Français. Les Romanesques: Comédie en trois actes, en vers.
Given at the Empire Theatre, New York,
February 24, 1901, by the American
Academy of Dramatic Arts, under the
name of " The Fantastics." Recently,
summer of 1911, widely given by a summer
company.

1895. April 5. Théâtre de la Renaissance. La
Princesse Lointaine: Pièce en quatre
actes, en vers. The part of Mélisande
was created by Mme. Sarah Bernhardt.

1897. April 14. Théâtre de la Renaissance.
La Samaritaine: Evangile en trois ta-
bleaux. The part of Photine by Mme.
Bernhardt. Several times revived during
Holy Week. Given by Mme. Bernhardt in
New York, December 8th, 1910.

1897. December 28. Théâtre de la Porte Saint-
Martin. Cyrano de Bergerac: Comédie
Héroique en cinq actes, en vers. The most

brilliant theatrical success of the dec-
ade. In the United States it was given
by Mr. Richard Mansfield at the Garden
Theatre, New York, October 3, 1898. In
London, at Wyndham's Theatre, with Mr.
Wyndham as Cyrano, April 19, 1900, it
did not seem to hit the public taste. It
has been given, in a translation by Ludwig
Fulda, in many cities of Germany and
Austria, and in New York also. Given in
French at the Garden Theatre, New York,
December 10, 1900, by Mme. Bernhardt
and M. Coquelin.

1900. March 15. Théâtre Sarah Bernhardt.
L'AIGLON: Drame en six actes en vers.
First given in the United States at the
Academy of Music, Baltimore, October 15,
1900. At Her Majesty's Theatre, Lon-
don, June 1, 1901. In French at the
Garden Theatre, New York, November 26,
1900, by Mme. Bernhardt and M. Coquelin.

1910. February 7. Théâtre de la Porte Saint-
Martin. CHANTECLER: Pièce en quatre
actes, en vers. First given in New York
at the Knickerbocker Theatre, January 23,
1911 (with Miss Maude Adams as Chantecler).

GERHARDT HAUPTMANN

(Unless especially mentioned, the place of production was Berlin)

1889. October 20. Lessing-Theater, under the auspices of the society Die freie Bühne. Vor Sonnenaufgang: Soziales Drama. The production of this play was an immensely exciting event, being regarded as a battle between the new school and the old. Like most of the plays following, it has been given at the Irving Place Theatre, New York.

1890. June 1. Lessing-Theater. Das Friedensfest: Eine Familienkatastrophe. This play had already appeared in the newspaper *Die freie Bühne*.

1891. January 11. Deutsches Theater. Einsame Menschen: Drama. This had been presented shortly before by the Freie Bühne. It has been given in German in New York, by Mr. Conried, of course, and in English as " Lonely Lives " at the Empire Theatre December 11, 1902, by the American Academy of Dramatic Arts.

1892. January 16. Deutsches Theater. College Crampton: Komödie in fünf akten.

1893. February 26. Die freie Bühne. Die
Weber: Schauspiel aus den vierziger
Jahren. The play was to have been given
at the Deutsches Theater, but was forbidden, and so not presented there till September 25, 1894. It has been given in Paris
as "Les Tisserands" at M. Antoine's
Théâtre Libre.

1893. September 21. Deutsches Theater. Der
Biberpelz: Eine Diebskomödie.

1893. November 14. Königliches Schauspielhaus. Hanneles Himmelfahrt: Traum-
dichtung in zwei Theilen. There were difficulties in regard to the presentation of this
play also. It appeared the next year at
the Théâtre Libre, Paris, and also at the
Fifth Avenue Theatre, New York.

1896. January 4. Deutsches Theater. Florian
Geyer. As first presented this play was a
failure, to the great chagrin of the author,
who had put his best work into it. He
revised it subsequently, and it was given
at the Lessing-Theater, October 22, 1904,
but I have not been able to get a satisfactory account of the nature of the revision
or of its success.

1896. December 2. Deutsches Theater. Die
versunkene Glocke. This play has been
Hauptmann's great public success; it at

once stirred up criticism and controversy
in Germany, and became more widely
known than anything he had yet done. It
was given to crowded houses by Frau
Agnes Sorma at the Irving Place Theatre,
New York, April 29, 1897, and afterward.
It did not appear in English, however,
until December 21, 1899, at the Hollis
Street Theatre, Boston, where it was presented by Mr. Sothern.

1898. November 5. Deutsches Theater. FUHR-
MANN HENSCHEL: Schauspiel in fünf
Akten.

1900. February 3. Deutsches Theater. SCHLUCK
UND JAU: Spiel zu Scherz und Schimpf.

1900. December 21. Deutsches Theater. MICHAEL
KRAMER.

1901. November 27. Deutsches Theater. DER
ROTE HAHN: Tragikomödie in vier Akten.

1902. November 29. Hof Burgtheater, Wien.
DER ARME HEINRICH: Eine deutsche Sage.

1903. October 31. Deutsches Theater. ROSE
BERND: Schauspiel in fünf Aufzügen.

1905. March 11. Lessing-Theater. ELGA.

1906. January 19. Lessing-Theater. UND
PIPPA TANZT.

1907. February 2. Lessing-Theater. DIE JUNG-
FRAU VOM BISCHOFSBERG.

1908. January 11. Lessing-Theater. KAISER
KARL'S GEISEL.

1909. March 6 $\left\{ \begin{array}{l} \text{Lessing-Theater, Berlin;} \\ \text{Hof Burgtheater, Wien.} \end{array} \right\}$
GRISELDA.

1911. January 13.   Lessing-Theater.   DIE
RATTEN: Berliner Tragikomödie.

HERMANN SUDERMANN

(Unless especially mentioned, the place of production was Berlin)

1889. November 27. Lessing-Theater. Die
Ehre: Schauspiel in vier Akten. Often
given in German. In English ("Honour")
at the Criterion Theatre, New York, January 26, 1905, by the American Academy
of Dramatic Art.

1891. November 5. Lessing-Theater. Sodom's
Ende: Drama in fünf Akten. This play
also has been widely given in German. The
first performance that I have noted in
English is "The Man and His Picture,"
Great Queen Street, London, March 8,
1903.

1893. January 7. Lessing-Theater. Heimat:
Schauspiel in vier Akten. This is the most
successful play that has been written of
late. It holds the stage better than anything even of Rostand or Hauptmann.
The character of Magda has attracted
the greatest actresses of the day—Mme.
Bernhardt, Signora Duse, Mrs. Patrick
Campbell, Mrs. Fiske, Mme. Mojeska, as
well as the chief German actresses. It has

been given almost everywhere, often under the name of " Magda."

1894. October 6. Lessing-Theater. DIE SCHMET-TERLINGSSCHLACHT : Komödie in vier Akten.

1895. November 11. Hof Burgtheater, Wien. DAS GLUCK IM WINKEL: Schauspiel in drei Akten.

1896. October 3. $\left\{\begin{array}{l}\text{Lessing-Theater, Berlin;}\\\text{Hof Burgtheater, Wien.}\end{array}\right\}$ MORITURI: Drei Einakter; TEJA; FRITZ-CHEN; DAS EWIG MANNLICHE.

1898. January 15. Deutsches Theater. JO-HANNES: Tragödie in fünf Akten und einem Vorspiel.

1899. January 21. Deutsches Theater. DIE DREI REIHERFEDERN : Ein dramatisches Gedicht in fünf Akten.

1900. October 5. Deutsches Theater. JOHANNES-FEUER. Given in English as " Fires of St. John," by Miss Nance O'Neil, at the Columbia Theatre, Boston, January, 1904.

1902. February 10. Deutsches Theater. Es LEBE DAS LEBEN: Drama in fünf Akten. Given by Mrs. Campbell at the Garden Theatre, New York, October 23, 1902. At the New Theatre, London, June 24, 1903.

1903. October 3. Lessing - Theater. DER STURMGESELLE SOKRATES: Komödie in vier Akten.

1905. October 7. Lessing-Theater. STEIN UNTER STEINEN : Schauspiel in vier Akten.

1906. October 6. Lessing-Theater. DAS BLU-
       MENBOOT.
1907. October 5. Hof Burgtheater, Wien. RO-
       SEN: Vier Einakter; DIE LICHTBÄNDER,
       MARGOT, DER LETZTE BESUCH, DIE FERNE
       PRINZESSEN. The first of these was not
       given with the others, being forbidden by
       the Censor.
1909. December 21. Königliches Schauspielhaus.
       STRAND-KINDER.

ARTHUR WING PINERO

(Unless especially mentioned, the place of production was London)

1877. October 6. Globe Theatre. Two Hundred a Year: A Comedietta in One Act.

1879. September 20. Lyceum Theatre. Daisy's Escape.

1880. June 5. Folly Theatre. Hester's Mystery: A Comedietta in One Act.

1880. September 18. Lyceum Theatre. Bygones: A Comedy in One Act.

1880. November 5. Theatre Royal, Manchester. The Money Spinner: A Drama in Two Acts. This was the first play of Mr. Pinero's to attract much attention. The production at Manchester was praised, and the play was brought to London, where it was given, January 8, 1881, by Mr. and Mrs. Kendal, Mr. John Hare, and others. It was considered worthy of note at the time by an accomplished critic that " Mr Pinero invents his own plots and writes his own dialogue," a remark very significant as to the English stage in 1880, a year in which "Forbidden Fruit" and "The Guv'nor" were the popular successes.

1881. July 27. Folly Theatre. IMPRUDENCE. Given at the Boston Museum, August 21, 1882.

1881. Dec. 29. St. James Theatre. THE SQUIRE. Given at Daly's, New York, Oct. 10, 1882.

1882. March 24. Court Theatre. THE RECTOR: A Play in Four Acts. Given at the Boston Museum, December 31, 1883.

1882. October 31. Toole's Theatre. BOYS AND GIRLS. Mr. Pinero was still on the stage and took a part in this play.

1883. July 30. Prince of Wales' Theatre, Liverpool. THE ROCKET: A Comedy in Three Acts. Given December 10, 1883, at the Gaiety Theatre, London.

1883. November 24. Haymarket Theatre. LORDS AND COMMONS: A Comedy in Four Acts.

1884. January 12. Globe Theatre. LOW WATER: A Comedy in Three Acts.

1884. Written but not presented till 1888 (p. 214). THE WEAKER SEX. It was to have been given at the Court Theatre, but was supplanted by the following piece.

1885. March 21. Court Theatre. THE MAGISTRATE: A Farce in Three Acts. This is a capital piece, though how good one can hardly appreciate without comparing it with some adaptations from the French of the same time. It was remarkably successful (ran for more than a year), so

that it determined the general line of the
Court Theatre for some time. It was
given at Daly's Theatre, New York, and
has since been presented all over Europe
and the English colonies.

1886. March 27. Court Theatre. THE SCHOOL-
MISTRESS: A Farce in Three Acts.

1886. October 23. Saint James' Theatre. THE
HOBBY HORSE: A Comedy in Four Acts.

1887. January 27. Court Theatre. DANDY
DICK: A Farce in Three Acts. Given at
Daly's Theatre, New York, October 5, of
the same year.

1888. March 21. Terry's Theatre. SWEET
LAVENDER. With the exception of " The
Magistrate," this is the most popular of
Mr. Pinero's earlier plays. Indeed, Mr.
Winter holds it to be " a thousand times
better than all his noxious analyses of
social sores." It was given at Daly's
Theatre, November 12, 1888, and has been
seen of late in New York given by Mr.
Terry, for whom it was originally written.

1888. September 28. Theatre Royal, Manchester. THE WEAKER SEX: A Comedy in
Three Acts. Written 1884. Given at
the Court Theatre, March 19, 1889, and
by the Kendalls during an American
tour.

1889. April 24. Garrick Theatre. THE PROF-
LIGATE: A Drama in Four Acts. This

play, which was the first strong piece of work in the kind wherein Mr. Pinero is now most distinguished, did not excite especial attention. It was not produced in this country until 1894, when people had become interested in the author through " The Second Mrs. Tanqueray."

1890. April 23. Court Theatre. THE CABINET MINISTER: A Farce in Four Acts.

1891. March 7. Garrick Theatre. LADY BOUNTIFUL: A Play in Four Acts. Not entirely successful, but given in the fall (November 16) simultaneously at the Lyceum Theatre, New York, and the Boston Museum.

1891. October 24. Terry's Theatre. THE TIMES: A Comedy in Four Acts. Of this play Mr. Pinero himself writes that " It lays bare no horrid social wound, it wrangles over no vital problem of inextricable perplexity."

1893. March 7. Court Theatre. THE AMAZONS: A Farcical Romance in Three Acts. Given at the Lyceum, New York, the next year.

1893. May 27. Saint James' Theatre. THE SECOND MRS. TANQUERAY: A Play in Four Acts. Given by the Kendals at the Star Theatre, New York, October 9, 1893. With this play Mr. Pinero begins to be considered seriously; it has been much discussed, and good critics have held it to be a great tragedy; a view which, I hope, (pp. 93, 94, 176, 195) is quite erroneous. Mrs. Patrick Campbell created the part of Mrs. Tanqueray, and the part did something of the sort in return. There have been French and Italian versions given in many places, but I do not hear of it in Germany.

1895. March 13. Garrick Theatre. THE NO-TORIOUS MRS. EBBSMITH. A very good play. Done by Mr. John Hare, at Abbey's Theatre, New York, December 23, 1895. Given September 22, 1899, at the Lessing-Theater, Berlin, under the name " Die Genossin."

1895. October 16. Comedy Theatre. THE BENEFIT OF THE DOUBT. Given at the Lyceum, New York, January 6, 1896.

1897. March 29. St. James' Theatre. THE PRINCESS AND THE BUTTERFLY; OR, THE FANTASTICS: A Comedy in Five Acts. Given at the Lyceum, New York, November 23, 1897.

1898. January 30. Court Theatre. TRELAWNEY OF THE WELLS: A Comedietta in Four Acts. Given at the Lyceum, New York, November 22, 1898.

1899. April 8. Globe Theatre. THE GAY LORD QUEX: A Comedy in Four Acts. Given in New York by Mr. Hare a year or so later. Also at the Lessing-Theater, Berlin, January 13, 1900, where it was pronounced by the only critic I have noted, " reichlich langweilig und . . . ein bedauerliches Zeichen für den Tiefstand des englischen Geschmackes." The remark is in itself an interesting sign of German taste.

1901. September 21. Garrick Theatre. IRIS: A Drama in Five Acts. Given at the Criterion Theatre, New York, September 23, 1902.

1903. October 8. Duke of York's Theatre. LETTY: A Drama in Four Acts and an Epilogue. Given at the Hudson Theatre, New York, September 12, 1904.

1904. October 9. Wyndham's Theatre. A WIFE WITHOUT A SMILE: A Comedy in Disguise. Given at the Criterion Theatre, New York, December 19, 1904.

1906. February 6. Saint James Theatre. HIS HOUSE IN ORDER: A Play in Four Acts. Given at the Empire Theatre, New York, September 30, 1906.

1908. May 9. Saint James Theatre. THE THUNDERBOLT: An Episode in the History of a Provincial Family. In Four Acts. Given at the New Theatre, New York, 1910.

1909. September 2. Saint James Theatre. MID-CHANNEL: A Play in Four Acts. Given at

the Empire Theatre, New York, January
31, 1910.

1911. January 24. Comedy Theatre. PRE-
SERVING MR. PANMURE: A Comic Play in
Four Acts.

Some translations or adaptations have been
omitted.

GEORGE BERNARD SHAW

(Unless especially mentioned, the place of production was London)

1892. Independent Theatre. WIDOWERS' HOUSES.

1893. { Written for the Independent } THE
Theatre, but not performed. }
PHILANDERERS; MRS. WARREN'S PROFESSION. The former was afterward given at the Court Theatre, February 5, 1907, and the latter by the Stage Society at the New Lyric Theatre, January 5, 1902. Given Hyperion Theatre, New Haven, October 27; Garrick Theatre, New York, October 30, 1905, for one night only.

1894. April 21. Avenue Theatre. ARMS AND THE MAN. Was also given by Mr. Mansfield at the Herald Square Theatre, New York, September 17, 1894. December 8, 1904, given at the Deutsches Theater, Berlin, as " Helden."

1894. Written for Mr. Mansfield, but not acted at the time. CANDIDA. Given at Princess Theatre, New York, December 9, 1903, and at the Court Theatre, on April 26, 1904. Given at the Königliches Schauspielhaus, Dresden, November 19, 1903.

1895. Written but not publicly given. THE MAN OF DESTINY. Given by the American Academy of Dramatic Arts at the Empire Theatre, New York, February 16, 1899, at the Neues Theater, Berlin, February 10, 1904, as " Der Schlachtenlenker," and at the Court Theatre, June 4, 1907.

1896. Written but not publicly given. YOU NEVER CAN TELL. Given at the Strand Theatre in 1900. Given January 9, 1905, at the Garrick Theatre, New York.

The above seven plays were published 1898 as " Plays Pleasant and Unpleasant."

1897. October 1. Bleecker Hall, Albany. THE DEVIL'S DISCIPLE. September 26, 1899, at the Princess of Wales' Theatre, and at the Berliner Theater, November 25, 1904, under the name " Ein Teufelskerl."

1900. Published. { CÆSAR AND CLEOPATRA. CAPTAIN BRASSBOUND'S CONVERSION.

Of these the former was afterward given at the Savoy, November 25, 1907, and the latter at the Court, May 27, 1906. They were given in New York, the former at the New Amsterdam Theatre, October 30, 1906; the latter, by Miss Ellen Terry, at the Empire Theatre, January 28, 1907.

1903. Published. MAN AND SUPERMAN. Given at the Hudson Theatre, New York, September 4, 1905.

1904. September 26. Berkeley Lyceum, New York. How He Lied to Her Husband.

1904. October. Court Theatre. John Bull's Other Island. Given at the Garrick Theatre, New York, October 10, 1905.

1905. November 28. Court Theatre, London. Major Barbara.

1906. November 16. Court Theatre. The Doctor's Dilemma. Under the name Der Artz am Scheideweg at the Deutschen Theater, Berlin, in 1908.

1908. May 19. Haymarket Theatre. Getting Married.

1909. July. Court Theatre. Press Cuttings. This was presented by the Civic and Dramatic Guild, but was shortly withdrawn on account of some objection to its political pleasantries. It was afterward presented with slight changes at Manchester, September 27, 1909.

1909. August 28. Abbey Theatre, Dublin. The Showing-up of Blanco Posnet.

1910. February 21. Duke of York's Theatre. Misalliance: A Debate in One Sitting.

1911. April 18. Criterion Theatre. Fanny's First Play.

STEPHEN PHILLIPS

1899. Published. PAOLO AND FRANCESCA: A Tragedy in Four Acts. Given at the St. James Theatre, March 7, 1902. New Amsterdam Theatre, New York.

1900. October 31. Her Majesty's Theatre, London. HEROD: A Tragedy. Given at the Vereinigten Stadttheater, Essen - Dortmund, September 29, 1905. Given at the Lyric Theatre, New York, October 26, 1909.

1902. February 1. Her Majesty's Theatre, London. ULYSSES: A Drama in a Prologue and Three Acts. Also given at the Garden Theatre, New York, September 14, 1902.

1904. Published. THE SIN OF DAVID. Given at the Stadttheater, Düsseldorf, September 30, 1905.

1906. January 29. His Majesty's Theatre. NERO.

1908. September 5. His Majesty's Theatre. FAUST. In collaboration with J. Comyns Carr.

1908. September 19. Adelphi Theatre. THE LAST HEIR. Adapted from " The Bride of Lammermoor."

1910. Published. PIETRO OF SIENA.

MAURICE MAETERLINCK

The dates given, except the last two, are those of publication. As the plays were not immediately performed, I have added a few dates of first performances in various countries, but the list is very incomplete.

1890. LA PRINCESSE MALEINE. Published: I have no record of any performance.

1892.
{ L'INTRUS.
LES AVEUGLES.
LES SEPT
PRINCESSES. }
The first two given by the American Academy of Dramatic Arts at the Berkeley Lyceum, New York, February 21, 1893, and January 18, 1894, respectively.

1893. PÉLLÉAS ET MÉLISANDE. Given at Prince of Wales' Theatre, London, June 21, 1898; at Victoria Theatre, New York, January 28, 1902; at Opéra Comique, Paris, May, 1902, as a lyric drama with music by Charles Debussy.

1894. { INTÉRIEUR.

ALLADINE ET PALAMIDES.

Both given at the Carnegie Lyceum by the American Academy, February 18, 1896.

LA MORT DE TINTAGILES. Given on the Sezessionsbühne, Berlin, November 12, 1900.

1896. AGLAVAINE ET SELYSETTE.

1901. ARIANE ET BARBE BLEUE: ou, La Délivrance Inutile. Conte en trois actes. Given, with music by Paul Dukas, at the Metropolitan Opera House, New York, March, 1911.

1901. SŒUR BÉATRICE. Miracle en trois actes. Given at the New Theatre, New York, March 14, 1910.

1902. May 17. Nouveau Théâtre, Paris. MONNA VANNA. Pièce en trois actes. Given at the Königliches Schauspielhaus, Munich, September 27, 1902. It was forbidden in London. In America it has been seen in German at the Irving Place Theatre, New York, and in English at the Manhattan Theatre, October 23, 1905. Also in Paris, 1910, at the Opéra as a lyric drama, with music by Fevrier.

1903. May 20. Théâtre du Gymnase. JOYZELLE: Pièce en cinq actes.

1908. September 30. Théâtre Artistique, Moscow. L'OISEAU BLEU. Given as THE BLUE BIRD at the New Theatre, New York, October 1, 1910.

1909. MARIE MAGDALENE.   Given at the Neue
     Stadttheater, Leipzig, March 12, 1910.
     At the New Theatre, New York, 1911.

INDEX

THE END